D1563268

LONG LINE RIDER

LONG LINE RIDER

The Story of Cummins Prison Farm

K Wymand Keith

McGraw-Hill Book Company

New York   St. Louis   San Francisco   London
Düsseldorf   Mexico   Sydney   Toronto

to Joyce, my wife
who encouraged me to write this book
and supported me while I was doing it

Although this book is based upon fact, all names are fictitious. This is to protect those few who, by necessity, have played a part in its unfolding but who may have been innocent—with the exception of Violet. She had nothing to hide.

LONG LINE RIDER

CHAPTER I

WE CAME into Arkansas through West Memphis and headed down U.S. 70 toward Little Rock. It was mid-October, ten o'clock in the morning —a gray, overcast, rainy day from the moment we got up. I told Violet that we should do well in Arkansas. I told her about the cotton pickers, the ridge runners and their low mentality. Then while I drove and watched the blackjacks and fields sweep by, she chewed bubble gum and studied the road map.

"There isn't a single place we can hit before we reach Little Rock, unless you want to try Forrest City."

She smacked her lips as she talked, and between phrases she blew bubbles. She was a pretty woman. She was neatly groomed and her dark eyes sparkled as she sat beside me there in the stolen automobile. But I had become tired of her. After our miles on the road together, I considered Violet a complete bore and little more than someone to be taken along to achieve my ends. I thought of her as an uneducated but rehabilitated slob, but I knew she possessed a quick mind. I knew that in tight spots, when a check-passing situation became too awkward, Violet would immediately be there with the proper words and the right psychology to extract us from it. The going got rough when we were alone. I was more than just bored, I think I was outright disgusted —particularly after three thousand miles of hearing her talk about giving ourselves up and straightening out and all that jazz. In such moments I had come to feel toward her as I would imagine an undertaker feeling toward one of his finished products. She was simply a part of my business.

Violet was, however, extremely difficult to ignore. If for no other reason, her gum chewing kept me reminded. As far as sex was concerned, there wasn't much left after three months and fourteen dozen hotel rooms. Even so, she was still a good-looking broad. And now she was well-dressed and minus the original crabs I had found her with back in Pennsylvania.

I had passed hot checks for her stylish clothes, and I had insisted that she bathe every day. For her I had even given a druggist a ten-dollar piece of worthless paper, just to be certain that she had an adequate supply of blue ointment.

She didn't appreciate it, though. She couldn't see the ever-present possibility of our raking in a small fortune and buy-ing a fancy bar or a chic nightclub. She was too busy popping her bubble gum and giving me generally a bad time.

I turned my head and looked at the clapboard houses and wet cotton fields along the highway. Damn a cotton field. And damn the fly-by-night sawmills tucked away in the valleys we passed. I had had my fill of both during my share-cropper upbringing in Oklahoma, and I wasn't about to do very much of any kind of hard work any more. I didn't have to. I had some eighteen sets of phony identification, and in my wallet I had a legitimate-looking title for the automobile I was driving. But somehow those wet cotton fields bothered me, as did the stooped pickers who were foolish enough to work in the rain. Without a word I swung the car to the muddy shoulder of the road and stopped about twenty feet from a bent figure slaving away at the far end of a cotton sack.

"Why are we stopping here?" Violet asked. "Why don't we go on to Forrest City and get something to eat?"

I didn't answer, but stepped from the car and walked around to the front. I stood for a moment and looked at the oily leaves and the red wine stems of the cotton plants. The rain had almost let up, and the bent figure had twisted around and was regarding me curiously.

He was an old man, with tobacco-stained face and gnarled hands. He wore bib overalls, and on his head was a flopped-down felt hat. Out beyond him there were other pickers, all standing now and staring at us.

"Why don't you come on, honey, and let's get something to eat?"

Slowly I walked to her side of the car. "Don't ever call me *honey* again. Just keep your mouth shut real tight or I'll take one of those whiskey bottles and break off the top and cut your throat with the jagged end." I turned and walked cautiously through the black gumbo toward the old man.

"Looks like you people have been having some bad weather down this way," I ventured, flipping the beads of water from an oily cotton leaf.

The old man nodded and shifted his frail body to a sturdier position. "What y'all stoppin' heah fer?"

"It wasn't because we wanted to. Who owns this property through here?"

The man pushed a handful of cotton into the sack. "What y'all wanta know thet fer?"

"Well, it's like this. I represent the Atomic Energy Commission and they have discovered uranium in these parts. They've sent me down here to buy the entire works and to set up a factory to process ore."

The old fellow blinked. "What's thet?"

"What's what? You mean uranium?"

He nodded.

"Oh, it's a kind of stuff the government uses to make atomic bombs. The people in Washington want to be three jumps ahead when the next world war begins so they can be first to blow up the goddamned planet. Now will you be so kind as to tell me who owns this mudhole?"

"Ah do, but ah ain't gonna sell it."

"Not for a million dollars?"

"Not fer nothin'," he stated emphatically. " 'Sides, ain't nobody got that much money noways."

"The government has."

"Not fer nobody down in these parts."

I changed the subject. "Looks like a pretty good cotton crop you've got there. Do you always pick it wet?"

"We put it to dry 'fore we gin it," he said defensively. "Takes too much money to hare pickers these days."

"Could you people use a few groceries?"

The old man seemed embarrassed. Immediately he began to pluck cotton from the taller stalks within his reach. "What fer?" he asked simply.

"Why hell, to eat, of course!"

"We got air own food." He squinted inquiringly at me. "What y'all askin' me thet fer?"

"It's part of the program," I invented. "The Special Services Division of the Atomic Energy Commission sent some food along for you folks to use while you're trying to make up your minds how much you want for this quagmire."

"We don't want nothin'," he tried to explain as I tiptoed back to the automobile, but I wasn't listening. I was thinking about the half-dozen boxes of canned food that Violet and I had shanghaied from supermarkets back up the road toward Nashville. My thoughts were diverted, however, when I saw Violet and the frown on her face.

"Get out here and unload these groceries," I commanded.

"I thought we were going to keep those and get us a little apartment."

"Look, just latch onto these boxes, one at a time, and swim out there where the old fellow is. Put each one down at his feet and say nothing. Then swim back. Now get moving, and don't drop your cud in the gumbo!"

One by one she carried the boxes out, and stumbled back. Each time she set one down I could hear the old man say something that sounded like *What fer?* He acted as though he wanted to urinate. And off to the north and above the trees a streak of lightning played crazily among the clouds. A moment later, thunder came—a slow heavy rumble that finally crashed and faded away in the distance. Then we were back in the automobile and Violet scraped furiously at her gold-flecked shoes.

"What in hell did you want to stop there for?"

"I have no idea," I answered. "Something about my childhood, I guess. Something about the cotton fields and the red wine stems that reminded me."

She stopped scraping and looked at me. "You know," she said, "you are the craziest man I've ever known." She edged closer to me. "But always I want to take care of you and make you happy."

And somehow the way she talked struck me as being unusually funny. I began to laugh. I thought of the wet cotton stalks and the old man and the boxes of groceries. I threw the car into low and spun from the muddy shoulder onto the hard surface. I shifted past second to high and pressed down hard with my foot. The heavy automobile careened dizzily down U.S. 70 toward Forrest City.

CHAPTER II

FORREST CITY was a dud. I still had a hundred dollars and by no means felt compelled to act fast. Had I been broke, I would have bounced a check or two on my way through, but under the circumstances everything about Forrest City was far too small—narrow streets, dingy stores, unreliable back roads in case of trouble. Along the main street I couldn't even find a decent café, and Violet was constantly asking me to stop for a bite to eat.

"Gosh, I'm hungry," she complained.

I reached below me and pulled a half pint of whiskey from beneath the seat. In rapid succession I took two long drinks. I then settled back for another lap of wet-weather driving.

Palestine. Goodwin. Wheatley. We passed Brinkley, but no café. When we reached Little Rock the first lights of early evening were beginning to appear. The rain had ceased and the sky was clear, and in the air was an autumn chill.

As we turned up the Arkansas River toward North Little Rock, I attempted to explain to Violet that maybe we should hit a few small business establishments before we checked in for the night. She didn't agree. She felt that we should eat first and then rest up for a few hours.

"You've still got that hundred dollars," she pointed out, "and when we're tired, like we are now, anything can happen."

The relationship between Violet and me had fallen to such a low level that everything she said irritated me. "Look," I countered, "these dumb hicks are a cinch for a quick buck. The way I see it, we can hit a few places for thirty or forty dollars each. Then if everything goes according to Hoyle and no heat develops, we can check in for the night at a hotel and be gone by the time the banks open tomorrow morning."

Violet plopped a bubble gum into her mouth and began to chew. "I'm hungry," she insisted, "and I'm too tired to work tonight anyhow."

"Look, you, whether you like it or not, we're playing this my way. If you want to be a good girl and help me in this one last city, then we'll quit this racket and go up north and settle down. I'll get a job and you can stay home and keep house and we'll have the happiest little love nest north of the Mason-Dixon line. If you keep complaining, however, I'm going to be forced to stomp your butt."

Violet stopped chewing and looked at me. Her eyes moistened and a sad but hopeful expression came over her face. I felt guilty at what I knew was a bald-faced lie. I wasn't about to settle down with anybody. Particularly Violet. I looked out the window and studied the service stations along the way.

Suddenly I swung the car to the right and parked on an off street that was lined with giant elms and shabby, unpainted houses. To my right and parallel to my parked position was a vacant lot. The first house ahead on that same side was a clapboard affair with a cluttered porch and a feeble light. The house directly behind us on that same side was completely dark, and across the street everything seemed to be pretty much in order. This was the spot I had looked for, a place on an off street where no resident would likely complain or wonder about our stopping.

I switched on the dashboard light and took a set of bogus identification papers from a marked envelope. For a driver's license I had what would pass as a driver's permit, listing my address vaguely as Route 1, North Little Rock. Also included in the papers from the envelope were other such items as a lodge card, a library card, a fishing license and a few homey tidbits like family pictures, dated letters and canceled envelopes. As I sorted through the articles and put them in their proper places in a special billfold, Violet studied the streets on a city map and plotted our getaway course.

"Highway 65 goes due north with plenty of off roads," she mumbled. "Do you want me to go with you or keep the motor running?"

"Go with me. Nobody's going to spot this crate buried in these elms. The station we're going to hit is around the corner and two blocks up. We'll use the old battery cable method and you will be Alice my wife. And—oh yes, the automobile we're driving is a 1947 Chevrolet." I took a long drink from a freshly opened fifth and tossed the bottle onto the back seat. "Now give me one of those universal blanks—no, make it two, just in case—and let's shove off."

The "We Fix It Service Station" was a two-pump, ethylene-regular pile of decrepit driftwood that I imagined had floated down the Arkansas River and come to rest at the base of the huge oak tree on a weeded lot. Inside the door of the one crowded room was a soda pop machine marked "Out'n Odor," and along the back was a broken glass case filled with oil cans, monkey wrenches, candy bars, and houseflies. A littered rolltop desk occupied a left-hand corner, and seated at the desk in a cloud of tobacco smoke was a slim man in bib overalls and rubber hip boots.

"Howdy, stranger," the man said, his Adam's apple going up and down. To Violet he nodded politely and rose to his feet.

"Stranger hell!" I objected. "You've called me that the last four times I was in here. How many times does a fellow have to come into your station before he's recognized?"

The man gulped and peered closely at me. "Wail now, ah didn't mean it like thet. How y'all been?" He offered his hand, then squinted at Violet. "Ah don't thank ah met the missy, though."

"No, I reckon you didn't, Slim. This lady is Alice, my wife."

"Wail now," he said simply.

"Is this the gentleman who fixed your tire the night of the storm?" Violet was broadcasting on fifty megacycles. She quickly added, "You shoulda seen him when he got home that night. He was soaked to the skin and sneezing his head off."

The man looked sad. He hooked his thumbs under the galluses of his overalls and shuffled his feet. "Wail now, maybe ah shoulda brung 'em on home, but thangs was so busy 'round heah."

"Oh, that's all right, Slim," I interrupted. "Maybe you can make it up to us now by selling me a battery cable for a forty-seven Chevy."

He glanced at a dusty array of fan belts, radiator hoses and

battery cables above his desk. "Groun' 'r pos'tive?" he asked.
"It'd be the flat one," I said.

"Groun'," he stated authoritatively, and reached up and pulled down a long one. "This'n ain't fer no forty-seven Chevy, but it'll work. Jus' put it on an' curl the middle 'round kinda." He stooped and rummaged through a cardboard box at the side of his desk. "Heah, take a mite o' this balin' wire an' sorta tie the middle part up to somepin' solid on the motor. Wheah y'all parked? Maybe ah'n run out an' he'p fix it while yer missy stays heah an' minds the store."

"I think I can get it okay, Slim. We're parked out a ways and we thought that since we had to come into town anyhow we'd do a bit of other shopping while we're here."

Violet picked up the cue. "Didn't you call Jack to come for us when we're finished shopping?"

"Not yet I haven't, but I will."

The man listened respectfully to the exchange between Violet and me. At last he said, "Wail, ah'n take y'all out an' he'p fix it."

"That's quite neighborly of you, Slim, but I think I can manage it all right. How much do I owe you?"

"Wail now," he figured aloud, "ah mostly charge fer takin' it down an' showin' it, but since y'all folks air buyin' . . thet'd be two sixty-one—call it two sixty even."

As he talked I had casually taken a universal blank from my billfold. I now sat down confidently at his rolltop desk and began to write. Violet kept up a running stream of conversation. She inquired concerning the health of the man's family. She asked him about his latest fishing escapades. She complimented him on his friendliness and his well-run service station. She smiled at him, she cajoled him, and she showed him a lucky charm she wore above her breasts. She even advanced a subtle invitation to him that could well have meant anything. "I'd simply love to go catfishing," she rambled on, "but my husband won't hardly take me anywhere." And then I had finished writing and I handed the check to him.

"I made this for thirty-five, Slim. As I said, Alice and I want to do a bit of shopping while we're in town and I'm caught without ready cash."

Calmly he took the piece of worthless paper and scanned it. He then reached down and opened a drawer of his desk and brought out a shoebox filled with litter. "Y'all know," he said shyly, "all these papers air checks ah los' money on." He flipped through one of the larger bundles as a banker might flip through a sheaf of hundred-dollar bills. "Ah ain't cashin' no checks fer nobody."

"You what!" I exploded. "Are you trying to tell me that you don't think my check's any good?"

"No—no," he assured me, "ah ain't sayin' thet atall. Yer check is prob'ly as good as gold. Ah jus' ain't cashin' no checks fer nobody, not even fer my own brother 'r mother." He untied the dirty twine string of one bundle. "Look at thet." He pointed to the checks. "All sorts o' reasons why they won't cash."

I reached over and spread the untied bundle across the desk. All sorts of reasons indeed, I mused. Overdrawn accounts. Insufficient funds. Suspected forgeries. Return for better identification. No account. There were light green checks printed on high quality paper. There were pink checks, trimmed and edged and as official-looking as any college degree. There were long checks and short checks and a narrow one marked *Certified*. There were checks bearing such unlikely signatures as C. U. Later and I. Screwedu. And there were checks like the one I was offering, quite meaningless and indefinite and without even a bank specified in the space intended for that purpose.

The man cleared his throat. "As ah were sayin', ah ain't cashin' no checks." He then grinned mischievously. "Ah'n tell y'all wheah to go, though." He walked to the door and pointed down the street toward the opposite side. "See thet station down theah? Wail, they cash checks durn nigh all the time."

"Look, Slim," I said indignantly, "as much as I've traded with you, and you don't want to cash one simple damn check for me. If that is the way you feel about me and my wife, I won't do any more business with you."

"Wail now," he drawled, "they ain't no call to get mad." He rubbed his chin and became thoughtful. "Since y'all ain't buyin' ah reckon y'all owe me a quarter fer showin' the cable."

That, I considered, was the last straw. Momentarily my emotions got out of hand and I stood there—undecided, frustrated, and plain damn hot under the collar. I recovered quickly, however. What had happened to my check-passing psychology that I would let a simple Arkansas idiot like this man get me down? Perhaps I should quit passing checks and begin picking cotton . . .

"If y'all ain't got the quarter the missy can leave 'er neck charm."

I laughed. I reached into my pocket and extracted a twenty-five-cent piece. "Business is rough on all fronts these days," I said. Then I looked directly into his twinkling eyes. "Here's your quarter, ol' buddy. May all your battery cables turn to pure gold."

CHAPTER III

VIOLET and I left Little Rock with two full buckets of fried chicken and another fifth of bonded whiskey. Due to operating expenses, we had less money than we had had upon entering the city, and I was in a bad mood.

We drove north on 65 and turned left at Conway. It was nine o'clock when we passed through Morrilton, and a full moon was peeping over the scrub oaks to the east. Apparently there had been no rain in that part of Arkansas, and the night seemed a little warmer. As we drove along an occasional cottontail rabbit darted into the bright light of the automobile and became confused. I swerved to miss each one, and thought of the slim man and his collection of hot checks. Violet fiddled with the radio and popped her bubble gum.

"A penny for your thoughts," she chirruped, and almost fell through the windshield when I suddenly put on the brakes and swerved to miss another rabbit. "Damn," she said, and straightened her dress around and beneath her bare legs. "I used to go with a boy who ran over every creature he saw on the road. One time he even ran head-on into a rhinoceros that escaped from a zoo and wouldn't move out of the way."

"That's nice," I said. "He must have been a real bright bastard."

"Naw," she confided, "he wasn't very. He later got killed in a car wreck. He wanted me to marry him and I guess I would have if he hadn't got killed."

"Imagine that."

"I've had men who wanted to marry me," she said defensively. "Lots of them."

"They must have been drunk."

"No, they weren't drunk," she flared. "They were nice guys back in Pennsylvania." After a moment she edged closer to me and regarded her image in the rear-view mirror. "I could get married any old time I wanted to."

"No doubt you could," I conceded. "Gravel Gertie did." I swung to miss another cottontail.

Violet moved back to her side of the automobile and pouted for a few miles. Suddenly she brightened. "When are we going to stop and eat the fried chicken?"

"Any time we can find a place to park," I said, and pulled the car off onto a dirt road that was narrow and lined with tall clover stalks. After a mile or so the clover broke away on my right and I swung into a partly wooded pasture that was unfenced and slanted gradually upward to the east.

"You're gonna get stuck out here. Why didn't you stop back there?"

"Look, don't tell me how to drive or where to stop. Just keep your advice to yourself and get me that whiskey bottle off the back seat."

The place where I parked was beneath an oak tree and facing the rising moon. Ahead of us at the far edge of the pasture the tree line was shadowed and dark and indistinguishable against the bright upper background. As I uncorked the whiskey bottle and sat for a moment reluctant to taste the first drop, I asked Violet absently, "Do you believe there's really a man in the moon?"

"I don't know. What do you believe?"

"Hell, I don't know. I asked you. There's nothing true that we don't believe in. If I believe there's a man in the moon, then there is. If I don't, there isn't. I prove this every time I go in to cash another check. If I think I'm going to succeed, I do. If I have doubts, I don't. It's that simple."

"Then I believe there's a man in the moon. I believe it because you do." She moved closer.

"Hey now, I didn't say I believe there's a man in the moon. I didn't say any such thing. So get those buckets out of the back seat and let's eat." I downed a long drink of whiskey.

Violet stuck her bubble gum under the dashboard and moved the fried chicken from the back seat and spread it between us. "They didn't give us but two little napkins," she fussed. "Damn, there's a lot of chicken here."

"Supposed to be three," I said between pulls on the whiskey bottle. "One and a half in each bucket."

"What piece do you want?"

"I like the gizzards."

"Ugh," she said girlishly. "We never did even cook those."

"By cracky, Mamma did. Pa wouldn't have eaten his dinner without chicken gizzards."

"What was it like where you grew up? I mean—well, you've told me some things, but what was your mother and father like and the farm where you lived?"

I belched. "There really isn't much more to tell. Mamma was Pentecostal and religious as all get out, and Pa was Baptist and drank moonshine whiskey. It was back in Depression days in eastern Oklahoma and we all just about starved our rear ends off."

Violet tore off a huge mouthful of chicken. "I don't even remember my mother. She left Daddy when I was two. But she didn't have any religion like your mother."

"I should hope not. Besides, I don't see anything so important about religion. The whole damn works is as phony as these checks I pass."

"Why do you keep passing them?"

"What's that got to do with religion? One moment you're talking about religion and the next moment you're trying to reform me. Just get off that kick. Where religion is concerned and check passing and any other thing, the only god I believe in is money—pure, sweet, unadulterated money. With that I can buy anything I want, even religion." I downed another shot of whiskey.

"Don't you really believe in anything else? You must believe in something other than money. You gave that old man those groceries and you wouldn't run over those little rabbits crossing the road."

"How many times do I have to tell you to get off my back. Now eat your goddamn chicken and leave me alone."

Violet remained silent for a long time. The only sounds in the automobile were those of her ripping and tearing at the fried chicken and the whiskey sloshing in the uncorked bottle. An acorn fell from the oak tree and landed on the metal top of the car, and a whippoorwill called from somewhere deep in the woodland. Violet stopped chewing for a few seconds. "What was that?" she asked, wide-eyed.

"An acorn and a whippoorwill."

Satisfied, she continued to eat. "Are we going up north now and settle down?"

"I dunno," I answered, feeling a bit drowsy.

"You said we would after Little Rock."

I straightened up in the seat. "Yeah, I say a lotta things I don't mean." I took a long drag from the whiskey bottle.

Violet rolled down her window and threw out a handful of chicken bones. She stopped eating and wiped her fingers on a soiled napkin. "You said that after we hit Little Rock we would head north and settle down. You said we'd get us a little apartment and you'd get a job." She twisted around in the seat and looked at me. "I would be a good wife and keep the house clean for you. I'd love you and help you do anything you wanted to do. I could even get a part-time job myself and work for a while."

"You know what you remind me of?" I took another drink. "You remind me of an old cow we used to have back in Oklahoma. That heifer could eat all day, and when she wasn't eating she was chewing her cud. Just like you chew that goddamn bubble gum."

"Then you didn't mean what you said?"

"Sure I meant what I said. We're headed north, aren't we? Goddamn what I said anyhow. I've already told you I don't mean a lot of things I say. Goddamn religion and goddamn society and every other stinking thing that goes with it. And goddamn you and your everlasting talk about love and marrying and settling down and all that crap." I opened the car door and stumbled drunkenly out. I staggered to the back and opened the trunk and took out a jack handle. "Goddamn the whole filthy world and everything in it!" I was screaming now, and beating the car. I smashed the back glass and ran crazily around the automobile breaking each window I came to. "Damn a god and a bitch that's always talking about one." I stood at the front of the car and beat down the hood with the jack handle. Blow after blow I landed upon the heavy metal. I beat the hood down to the motor and threw the handle at the cracked windshield. Saliva bubbled at my mouth and my right hand became wet with blood from a glass wound. Then I slid down on my knees and passed out in the grass and weeds of the pasture.

CHAPTER IV

THE TWO people who drove from the wooded pasture next morning were a sorry sight. I needed a shave, my shirt was bloodstained, and my trousers were wrinkled and looked as though I had slept in them for many months. My head ached, and there was a dry, funky taste in my mouth. And the wound in my right hand was also beginning to throb. Violet had bound a dirty handkerchief across my thumb and around the palm, but as I drove and looked at the useless bundle upon the steering wheel I realized that I would have to have my hand treated and bandaged before I could go much farther. Violet sat quietly and stared straight ahead. On her side of the automobile the windshield was merely cracked and splayed with one big cloudy spot. On my side, however, the glass was knocked out completely and the windshield wiper was bent forward toward the nose of the car. There was no rain and little wind that morning, and luckily so. Every other window in the car was gone, and glass littered the back seat. Violet and I had both made a halfhearted attempt to sweep the car out and to straighten things up, but there was little use. Brown chicken bones still lay in the cracks of the floorboard, and all the interior smelled of whiskey and soured vomit. The automobile was a junkpile. It scraped beneath the battered hood and rattled around the window frames of each door. I looked at the temperature gauge and saw that the engine was beginning to heat up. In my bacchanalian frenzy I had apparently damaged the fragile copper tubing that circulated the water through the radiator. The car coughed and spit tiredly.

"What'll we do if we meet a patrolman?" Violet asked, suddenly coming alive and scraping around in the glove compartment.

"That's the least of my worries," I said absently. "A highway patrolman wouldn't dare stop us. He'd be afraid to."

"Maybe we should ditch all the phony papers in case one does."

"I'm not worried about that. The only thing a patrolman would do if he spotted us in this heap is take to the woods screaming. What I need is some water for this crate."

"Why don't you try one of these bar ditches along the road?"

"All right," I said, "I'll do that. And meanwhile you can get off your rear end and patch up the radiator tubing with a wad of that chewing gum."

"It won't stay in," she declared.

"Fine and dandy, then let it stay out. All this jalopy can possibly do is cloud up a bit and come to a screeching halt."

And cloud up it did. As Violet and I entered Russellville huge puffs of white steam issued from the rattletrap we were riding in. The steering wheel squeaked and was difficult to turn toward the right side. "Know what I'm going to do?" I asked Violet as I wrestled the automobile around a corner and parked in front of an old hotel-restaurant. "I'm going into this haunted-looking rathole and register for a room with a big bathtub and enough running hot water to scald every fish in the Arkansas River. And you are going to find a liquor store and purchase a fifth of good whiskey. And don't be gone all day," I called after her as she slid obediently from the front seat and headed up the street. I took my bags from the trunk and entered the building.

"Did y'all have a n'axydent 'r somepin'?"

The clerk was an old woman with two teeth. The counter she stood behind was littered with pay-in-advance notices, check-out schedules, coffee stains, and a rusty metal bell with a cardboard sign that said: "Rang fer Manager." The crone stared intently, first at my bloodstained shirt and then at my injured right hand.

"Not exactly, we didn't, ma'am. You see, it was like this. I'm traveling with my wife and we fell out of a cellar. Of course, she made out a little better than I did. She landed on top. Now do you have a room with a bath you can rent to a couple of poor tired travelers?"

"My—my," the old woman clucked. "Ah never heard o' anybody fallin' out'n a cellar." She looked up a shabby staircase and said politely, "Ah gotta room fer y'all but they ain't no bath. Y'all hafta go 'cross the street to thet service station on the corner to wash up. We got a private 'greement with them."

"My dear lady, do you mean to tell me that you have no place in this hotel to bathe?"

"They will be soon, when we get air plumbin' in. Right now we ain't got no runnin' water atall."

"What do you do about your commode, flushing it and all?"

She seemed embarrassed. "If y'all mean air toilet, we got one out'n back." She indicated a doorway. "Y'all hafta go through theah an' out pas' the mulberry bush. Ah jus' took a fresh bundle o' papers out an' swept up the place, so they ain't no worry 'bout it not bein' clean 'r anythang." She passed a cane-bottomed chair over the counter to me. "Y'all can prop this 'neath the door handle in yer room. Can't seem to keep no keys 'round heah."

I took the chair and started up the staircase.

"Firs' door to the left," she called after me. "Need anythang, ah'm Ma."

I opened the door and walked into the room. It was easy to describe. It had one bed, four walls, a floor and a ceiling and one window. And that was all.

Violet came in. "This is Pope County," she began, but I interrupted her.

"I don't care what county it is. Didn't you get anything to drink?"

"No."

"Why not?"

"It's a dry county."

I fell back on the lumpy mattress and grabbed my forehead. "Oh boy," I groaned, "that's just what I need. A stinking county that doesn't sell booze!" Presently a thought crossed my mind. "How about beer?" I asked hopefully.

"Nothing," Violet said.

The old woman appeared in the doorway. "Y'all can get a drank at Dardanelle. Thet's jus' fi' miles 'cross the Arkansas River. Thet's Yell County."

"What about right now?" I countered. "I need a drink in a bad way. I'm in a helluva shape."

The crone looked with interest from Violet to me. She

leaned closer and almost whispered. "Y'all ain't no cops, air ya?"

I laughed. "No," I assured her, "I've been accused of everything else but not that. I'm no cop."

She seemed relieved. "Ah ain't accusin' nobody o' nothin', but y'all better be careful 'round this town." Again she lowered her voice. "Get ya a pint fer six dollars. Bottle an' bond. Good stuff."

"Grab it," I said, "and hurry back."

She stepped inside and closed the door. With her back to me she lifted the folds of her long skirt. When she turned, she handed a pint to me. Without a word I took out a five and a dirty one and handed them to her. She tucked the money inside the neck of her dress, then she opened the door and spoke loudly. "They got good food down theah, when yer ready to eat, at the rest'rant."

CHAPTER V

B Y FOUR o'clock on the day Violet and I arrived in
Russellville, we were scrubbed and dressed and
again looked civilized. Violet had gone to a drug-
store and brought back a bottle of Mercurochrome and a
package of bandages. Slowly and methodically she cleaned
and treated and bandaged the wound in my hand.

"You're a pretty good little doctor," I complimented her.
I was now relaxed on the bed and feeling the effects of the new
pint. "You know what? I was going to drop you back in
Little Rock, but I think I've decided to keep you around for
a while."

Violet finished the bandage and pulled down my sleeve.
"You should have a few stitches taken. You're going to take
a long time to heal up like that."

"Where did you learn so much about medicine?" I asked
dreamily.

"Really I don't know an awful lot. I worked at this hospital back in Harrisburg but I didn't do much doctoring. I

mostly emptied bedpans and changed sheets." She rolled toward me on the bed and propped herself on an elbow. "You were mean last night," she whispered softly.

"Yeah, I know." I pushed my injured hand beneath her armpit and up near her back. "But Daddy wasn't mean to you, was he?"

"No, 'sall right," she breathed. Her dark eyes were alive and glistened like new tar. She leaned closer and touched my cheek. "Let me take you up north and make you happy."

"Is that what you really want? I'd be a pretty difficult hombre to tame."

"I don't think so. You've just got to not be angry at everybody and let me take care of you."

"All right," I said, pulling myself away from her and to my feet. "I've got some blanks on a Conway bank. And I've got some special identification that certifies me as a diamond dealer. There's a jewelry store in Dardanelle, a small hick place where nobody knows much of anything about what's going on. We'll go over there and hit that one spot for a few hundred dollars' worth of unsalable stones. These are diamonds that have a high carbon content and little or no market value through retail stores. For a few dollars we can get a handful, and every Tom, Dick and Harry in every bar through Oklahoma will buy one and pay well. These goofballs in taverns and bars don't really look closely at anything. They'll even buy zircon, thinking they're getting the real McCoy, and I'll mount each diamond we get in a cheap setting, and after that one good haul we'll go. We'll even tear up our identification, except for what we need on that one job. Violet, if you will help me I guarantee that I will make you the happiest woman on the face of this earth."

Violet had been sitting quietly listening to my every word. Finally she said, "What'll we do about the car?"

"Leave it where it is. We'll get a taxi to Dardanelle, and we'll get one back. Other than stripping that car of all papers and wiping away a few prints, we'll leave it parked. Eventually the city will come and tow it away, and some Arkansas idiot in some junkpile of a used car lot will pick it to pieces and sell each part for nine times what it's actually worth. But you and me, we'll be long gone. What do you say? Are you with me?"

Violet stood up and put on her coat. She gathered up a few items and then stopped. "Will we be coming back here?"

"Only to get our belongings and to catch a train north. We should be packed, though, and ready to move out." I opened the door and stepped into the hallway. The old woman was standing there. "Do you live in front of this door?" I asked her. At the same time I wondered how much she had heard.

"They's a cab right down the street. Ah'll take care o' yer belongin's." The old woman looked knowledgeable as all get out. I stood for a moment undecidedly. I did have something on her. She couldn't afford to say much, even if she had heard anything.

"All right," I said, "you do that." And to Violet, "Come on, kid, let's hit 'em."

The taxi turned out to be a dilapidated pile of junk that would have made the automobile Violet and I drove into town look like a Cadillac. It had no hood, and the rear end rode high in the air as though it were pushing the rest of the car forward. I noticed that a gasoline smell permeated the vehicle, and before I lit up a cigarette I thought for a long time.

"Dardanelle? What y'all wanta go over theah fer?" The driver could have made Violet ashamed of her gum chewing any old day. He chewed spearmint, peppermint and grape-nut. One after the other he plopped the pieces into his mouth. Finally he squirmed and hacked and spat out the car window. He rubbed his hands on the thighs of his trousers and started the motor. "Had a man an' a woman went over to Dardanelle one time. They jus' went over to raise Cain like y'all air doin'. They got took fer ever'thang they had." He looked warningly at me from the corners of horn-rimmed glasses. "If y'all got any big money y'all better not take it over theah." He smacked his lips and chewed rapidly. "Nope, y'all shore better not. They took thet couple. Course, thangs mighta changed since then."

The taxi pushed its way up the creosote bridge and thumped across.

"Where's the best place to go for a drink in Dardanelle?"

"Take y'all down to the Bucket o' Blood. Course, don't get me wrong. They ain't all bad over heah. They's some good places. This Bucket o' Blood, fer instant, ain't bad in theah atall. People don't cause no trouble, they ain't gonna say nothin'. Course, y'all bein' clean an' all, they ain't no one gonna bother ya. Jus' min' yer own bus'ness an' they'll take up fer y'all when trouble starts."

"Do you want to wait and be ready to take us back, in case they start shooting before we get through the door?"

He frowned. "They ain't gonna shoot at nobody lessen y'all starts trouble. Jus' go in an' tell the bartender Joe from Russellville sent ya. Y'all be welcome." He plopped another assortment of gum into his mouth and added, "Ah can't wait nohows, lessen y'all wanta hare the cab fer all night. But they's a cab heah in Dardanelle." He pulled up in front of the Bucket o' Blood and stopped. "Jus' tell 'em Joe from Russellville sent ya— thet'll be fi' dollars."

I paid the driver and accepted his further assurances. Then I turned and looked up the dusty street. Dardanelle was a small place—a very small place indeed. Along each side of the streets were hitching rails, and behind them were boardwalks. Noise issued from the Bucket o' Blood and, as Violet and I stood on the street in front of it, a beer bottle came through the swinging doors and splattered against a post to our right. A drunk staggered out and stood sullenly a few feet away on the boardwalk. With an eye on him and another on passersby, I noticed that practically everyone who came along turned and looked inquiringly at us. The drunk stood and glared for what seemed to be several moments. At last he gave up and stumbled to the edge of the boardwalk. He fumbled at his trousers and, failing to find the fly in time, broke wind loudly and urinated down both legs.

"Welcome to the Bucket o' Blood!" someone shouted as Violet and I entered the smoke-filled room. "A drank fer the house!" another man yelled, and several people pushed forward and around us. The bartender echoed the order and began setting drinks on one end of the bar. "Thet'll be eight twenty," I heard him say, and Violet nudged me with her elbow.

"He's talking to you."

I started to object but decided that I had better not. "Joe the Grinder sent us," I said to the bartender.

He pushed his face close to mine. "Look, bud, whata ya trying' to do, act funny?"

"He means Joe from Russellville," Violet corrected.

"Whyn't ya say so!" the bartender sang out. Then over his shoulder he yelled: "Joe from Russellville sent these folks! C'mon, you bums, pay fer yer dranks—forty cents, heah's yer change—thirty-fi'—ah ain't got no change fer a ten-dollar bill. If y'all ain't got no money smaller'n thet, get out." He looked at Violet and me. "Ah ain't talkin' to you folks. Heah, have one on the house."

Diamond Cutter's Jewelry Store was two blocks down from the Bucket o' Blood and on the same side of the street. The blocks weren't really blocks, but one long continuation of hitching rails and shabby fronts. As Violet and I approached the store, I stopped on the boardwalk a few doors away and told her to wait outside and to watch for any signs of trouble. "The Dardanelle taxi is around the corner, and we can be in it and out of town before these hicks ever know what is taking place." I entered the store.

A slim, anemic-looking little man with arms akimbo was standing inside. He wore a blue pin-striped suit that was long out of style and far too small. His hair was slicked down with some barnyard version of a pomade, and on his arms two inches below each elbow he wore wristwatches—bright and shiny watches that were ticking as loudly as a Big Ben at a countdown.

"May I be of service to you?" he asked politely, bowing.

I was struck by the absence of any accent. "I certainly hope so," I answered with an air of affectation that matched his own. "I'm interested in any unsalable diamonds you happen to have on hand. Nothing so very large, but only those which still have some commercial value."

"Surely, one moment please." He went to the back of the store and opened a vault. Soon he returned with a tray bearing two chamois-skin bags of unset diamonds. "Some of these may be rather large, but there are others we have had on hand for some time. Are you a dealer?"

"I am indeed," I said, and flashed my card.

"Then you are well aware that these diamonds are far from perfect." He glanced at my injured hand.

"Aren't all diamonds," I answered, and saw that he approved. I fumbled in a side pocket of my coat and added, "Have you a loupe? I seem to have left mine in the automobile."

He reached below and handed me one. "I think you will find that all these are rather imperfect."

"How much would you want for them?" I held the loupe and studied a few of the stones.

"The larger ones also?"

"All but these." I pushed a couple of the larger diamonds to one side.

"You may have them for ten per cent above cost . . . say, five thousand dollars."

"I'll give you four." I continued to study various stones.

"I'm sorry, sir, but I'm in no position to barter. Five thousand dollars is the very best price I could possibly quote you on these diamonds."

"Very well," I said finally, and took from my wallet the blank check I had picked up at Conway. As I wrote out the check with my left hand, the little man stood with his arms crossed and observed me impassively, his watches ominously ticking away the time. When I had finished he took the check and glanced briefly at it. He then folded the worthless paper and held it between two fingers.

"Thank you for your patronage, sir. Please stop in again when you're over this way." He again bowed politely.

"Let's get out of here," I said to Violet as I passed her on the boardwalk. I hurried around the corner and spoke to the taxi driver, who was sitting idly and reading a Hot Springs racing sheet.

"Get in," he said happily. He swung the taxi from its parked position and around the corner. As we passed the jewelry store I saw the little man come out on the boardwalk and stare after us. The driver burst into song. *"It's a long ways down the river when yer travelin' all alone . . ."*

Violet moved closer to me and the chamois-skin bags pinched my leg.

"Drop us at Ma's hotel down by the train station."

"Will do," the driver answered merrily. *"Oh, how can she go with ya when you'll be a long time gone?*— two fifty!"

I handed him three ones. "Why do you charge only two fifty from Dardanelle but Joe from Russellville charges five?"

He sang the words as he answered me. *"Joe from Russellville knows his trade, but the dif'rence 'twixt us is the way we're made."* He slammed the door and headed the taxi back toward Dardanelle.

Without a word Violet and I walked into the hotel. Ma followed us to our room. "Take this fer a present from me." She handed me a pint of bonded whiskey. "But y'all kiddies better hurry. They'll be heah any minute."

And she was right.

As Violet and I walked from the hotel with our suitcases, whiskey bottles and everything else we owned, all hell broke loose. The cars came in from every direction. There were city police and county sheriffs and state officials. There were cars with white sides with decals painted upon the doors. Some of the cars were open-topped, with men standing and holding guns. Where they all came from I did not know, but there were farmers and merchants and dogs on leashes, and even a small boy with a drawn slingshot.

"Stop wheah ya air! Drop them suitcases! Hands over yer head!"

I heard them shouting but none of the things they were saying seemed to register upon my mind. I dropped the suitcase I was carrying and felt the brown paper bag with the whiskey bottles slip from under my arm. I heard the bottles shatter on the concrete, and instantaneously another part of my being took over. It was almost as though a second person were sending messages to my every muscle and demanding that they act. And it was that part of my being that caused me to slip my wounded right hand under my coat and attempt to pull out the .25 automatic I carried there.

Violet screamed. "No—no! Don't shoot!" And I knew that she was screaming at me and for my safety. But there was no need for her concern. My wounded right hand would not respond and strong arms pinned me down and held me in vise-like braces.

"Take his gun! Take his gun!" someone kept saying. "We got 'em! We got 'em!" And then I felt handcuffs biting into my wrists and I relaxed. I knew that for me it was all over.

"We'll take 'em to the jail in Dardanelle. You'n put her up heah fer the night." The commands were sharp and crisp and heavily accented. "Wire Little Rock an' Memphis thet we got 'em."

Two fat deputies pushed me into the back seat of an automobile and two sat up front. "Y'all don't wanta pull no gun out aroun' heah, boy. Yer lucky ya ain't dead."

I tried to see what was happening to Violet, but all I could tell was that somewhere in the melee she was screaming and kicking and struggling toward the automobile I sat pinned in. Presently the crowd opened up and I saw a deputy clip her jaw. Her body went limp and I heard them laugh and saw them toss her half-naked body into the back seat of another car. Someone opened the doors of the battered automobile we had driven into town.

"Search it good," the sheriff ordered. "Look under the dashboard an' all 'round."

"Damn," a city policeman complained, "they's 'nough chewin' gum stuck under this dash to start a fact'ry!"

Red lights flashed, but the crowd had calmed down. They seemed satisfied that we were secure. They stood around and looked into the automobile, their faces stern and hard and unrelenting. I tried not to look at them. I looked at the street in front of the hotel where I might have died. I saw on the concrete where the law had pinned me down a piece of bubble gum and a little bit off and to one side I saw the wrapper. Apparently Violet had been unwrapping a new piece of gum as we left the hotel. I saw Ma standing against a far wall, and she shook her head sadly. I could not look at her. My gaze went back to the sidewalk and the bubble gum wrapper, and I saw that a light breeze had caught the small piece of paper and was moving it down the walk toward the curb. It was the same place on the curb where the amber fluid from the broken whiskey bottles trickled over.

CHAPTER VI

As THE car pulled out of Russellville and onto the main route to Dardanelle, the driver kept looking into the rear-view mirror, sometimes at me and sometimes behind us at another car following. One of the deputies sitting by me kept shifting his weight and adjusting a holstered gun at his side. The questions never ceased.

"Wheah ya from? Ever been in trouble before? Wheah'd ya steal thet car? Pass any hot checks in Little Rock? Y'all thank yer a smart bastard. We gonna work you over when we get you in jail."

On and on they rambled, and one held his face close to mine and he stank to high heaven. I remained quiet for a while and would not answer even the most sensible questions. Finally, however, I had stood it as long as I could and I blurted out: "You people know where I'm from. I heard you mention Little Rock and Memphis when you were arresting me. Obviously you know that the car is stolen and that I've been passing hot checks. Now the only thing I have to tell you is my name. Beyond that I have nothing to say until I've consulted an attorney."

The deputy with the bad breath leaned closer and sneered. "Le'me tell y'all somepin', boy. Wheah yer goin' you ain't gonna need no 'torney. We got ya dead to right, an' we gonna make you wish you'd never been borned."

"What if the federal wants to take me on that hot car rap? That comes under the Dyer Act, you know."

The driver, who turned out to be the sheriff of Yell County, spoke. "Whyn't ya hit thet smart sonofabitch in the mouth?" When no one did so, the driver continued. "No federal's gonna get you fer a long time, boy. When we get through with you they won't be much o' anythang left fer no federal."

The deputies laughed.

"What'll you do with Violet?" I asked. "She had no part in any of this."

"She were with you, weren't she? An' don't thet make 'er a n'access'ry? You know so much 'bout law an' all." It was the sheriff who spoke.

I remained silent and looked at the town I was entering for my second time.

"Y'all get out an' stan' back theah on each side," the sheriff said. As he spoke he indicated to the two deputies beside me the rear of the automobile and the dark area below the trees. "Me an' Buck'll take 'em on up an' you'n foller." He turned to me. "C'mon, boy, we gotta nice safe place fer ya, but y'all can't cash no checks theah." They all laughed again and the sheriff and his deputy led me up the steps of the courthouse, each with an arm locked through mine on either side.

The interior of the courthouse was clean and polished. The steps leading up to the second floor were framed by mahogany banisters that were scarred and pitted but shined with a high gloss.

"We'll lock 'em up heah fer the rest o' the night an' maybe take 'em to Danville tomarra."

Roughly they pushed me into a room and locked a heavy steel door. Then they left me alone and, once the sound of their footsteps had died away beyond the bottom of the stairway, the dark room became quiet and foreboding. Immediately I went to the barred, half-opened window and squinted into the night, but because of the deep courthouse shadows I could see nothing. The breeze from the river felt cool on my face, however, and I stood there for a long time. At last I became aware of the handcuffs biting my wrists. The backwoods posse who had brought me over and locked me up hadn't even bothered to remove them.

On October 17 dawn came late to the town of Dardanelle. The sky was now overcast and a light rain was beginning to fall. I hadn't slept much in my cramped quarters, and what little I had managed was accomplished by lying on my right side on the iron slats of a wall bunk. My wrists throbbed painfully and were badly swollen, and my injured hand was beginning to leak through the bandage Violet had placed around it so carefully. I looked out the window and saw that next to the courthouse was a weeded lot. Beyond it were a few shabby buildings that were all but hidden in the heavy growth of river bottom timber. I examined the bars in the windows, only to see that they were dovetailed into the frame of the courthouse structure and were indeed solid. I looked around my small prison and saw that the walls were covered with marks. I examined the steel door and leaned quietly against it to test its strength. Failing to move it even a fraction, I turned again to the walls and absently read a few of the markings.

Presently I heard the jingling of keys and the sounds of many feet. I hurried to the bunk and sat down. A key turned in the heavy steel door and several deputies entered my cell. I started to get up but before I could do so one of them landed a blow to the side of my head.

"You sonofabitch, we gonna break you from suckin' eggs."

Blow after blow they hit me, and I felt the steel cuffs bite deeper into my arms. I staggered and fell back on the latticework of the bunk, but strong hands pulled me up and chopped at my face and my midsection. Desperately I attempted to hide my face with my shoulder, but the blows rained on the other side of my head and I felt my jaw sag hopelessly.

"Hol' it a minute. Le'me get in theah with 'em."

Vaguely I recognized the voice of the sheriff and saw him approach me. While deputies held me up with arms locked through my own, the sheriff took from his side pocket a lead-filled blackjack and struck me over the head. Time and again he hit me, and my head went down. Through blurred eyes I saw the blood on my shirtfront. *My blood,* I thought crazily, but the blows no longer hurt. I no longer felt the boots that kicked at my ribs as I lay on the floor by the iron bunk. Clouds came and went, and one sharp pain crossed my belly. And then that merciful built-in mechanism known as unconsciousness took over, and I dreamed of many things.

In my dreams I saw a bottle of bonded whiskey and an evil-looking man in a cotton field. I felt the car I was driving run into a concrete wall and jolt me painfully. I dreamed that they carried my helpless body to some room with bright lights and whiskered faces bending over me. I dreamed that a doctor combed my hair and a deputy asked him if I should have it slicked down with pomade. The room spun, and then went blank, and spun again. Toes nudged at me and voices commanded me to sit up. There were long periods of deep silences, then hours upon end of loud laughs and guffaws. The ceiling leaned to one side and then righted itself. I heard myself groan and I knew that I tried many times to turn over onto my right side, but something was holding my left leg and I lay back. I waited and dreamed, ugly dreams that were harsh and painful and made little sense. I ached and screamed in my half delirium and struggled for air. Then the clouds outside left my nightmarish mind and the sunlight streamed through the half-opened window.

"We ain't mad at ya, boy. We jus' wanted to learn ya a lesson. You corp'rate with us an' behave yerself an' you'll be all right."

I looked in the direction the voice came from and saw that the sheriff was addressing me. "What day is it?" I asked, for no particular reason.

"October twenty-first, but y'all don't need to worry none 'bout thet. You ain't goin' nowheah." The deputies behind him laughed, but this time the laughs were not so loud or enthusiastic.

"Y'all thank you'n pull yerself together 'nough to go over to Russellville? We gonna let you see yer girl frien'."

I tried to sit up, but the sheriff took hold of my right arm and assisted me. At the same time, a deputy unlocked the chain that was binding my left leg to the iron frame. I saw that my arms were free so I pushed my palms to my forehead. There were thick bandages around and under my chin, and a tight but elastic contraption held my rib cage.

"Jus' behave yerself," the sheriff repeated, "an' no one gonna hit ya no more."

Thank heaven for that! In my still half-crazed mind, the moment was a glorious one. I felt that I loved and trusted these men and that perhaps I had been wrong and they had been right after all. I took advantage of the sheriff's reassuring words to stand for a moment and to tell them to wait. I blinked dizzily, and felt giddy, but the strong arms of the deputies held me up. Then I found myself leaning toward a wall and trying to read the markings upon it. The sheriff and his deputies waited patiently.

"June, 1946," the marking declared, "I stole a calf. If anyone wonts to read about me I am wrote up in the Russellville newspaper fer the sixteenth. You will hear more from me. I will go down in the pages of Arkansas histery as one of its trully great outlaws."

A deputy giggled. "Looky heah, sheriff, what somebody wrote after thet." He read aloud, " 'You won't do it stealin' little ol' calves.' " They all guffawed.

"He shore won't," the sheriff said, slapping his thigh. "He shore 'nough won't!"

The trip back to Russellville was uneventful. The deputies sat crowded around me as though I were some savage killer, but I was now without handcuffs. My wrists were swollen and my head ached and my insides felt as though they were coming apart. The deputies talked and laughed and hooted, but somehow or other they seemed to have lost interest in me completely. They talked about fishing and about some crumb in a beer joint in Dardanelle, and about a fellow deputy who wasn't present but who apparently had been caught in a woman's bedroom with his trousers off. They ranted and raved and hurled obscenities at each other, but no one seemed to take offense.

"If you don't win this nex' election," someone was saying, "ain't none o' us gonna have no job."

"Who in hell's gonna dare vote ag'in me?" the sheriff laughed. "They ain't no damn Republican gonna do it, you'n be shore o' thet!"

"Are you gentlemen going to let me see an attorney?" I asked weakly.

The sheriff swung past Ma's place and down toward the jail. He looked in the rear-view mirror and studied me before he spoke. "Y'all ain't gonna start thet crap ag'in, air ya, boy?" When I did not answer, he added, "Y'all don't need no lawyer noways. Yer guilty as all sin." He pulled the car to the curb in front of a stone structure that I recognized as the Pope County jail. To the deputies around me he said, "Y'all don't need to pay him much mind. Jus' take 'em on in an' if he tries anything, shoot 'em."

"Whata we got heah?" a Russellville deputy asked as we approached the desk.

"We gotta wise bastard, but he's calmed down some now. He didn't like air hospitality an' we had to he'p 'em decide thet he wanted to stay. Tried to make a break from us."

The Russellville deputy looked at me a second time and shook his head. "Crime don't pay, do it, boy? Crime jus' don't pay."

"Ah called Albert this mornin' an' he said brang the prisoner on over. You'n put 'em up in a cell next to hern an' let 'em get reacquainted ag'in. We ain't fed 'em yet. Ah don't thank he's eatin' much nowadays noways."

The deputies led me up another stairway and down a hall. To my right the wall was blank with yellow paint peeling off, but to my left bars formed a side for the hallway and in one cell as we passed I saw Violet. She lay on a mattress and whimpered and didn't notice me as they shoved me on. The barred door they opened for me was at the end of the hallway, at a right angle to the front of the cell that Violet occupied.

"What have you done to her?" I asked the deputies as they locked me in.

"They ain't nothin' wrong with 'er, boy. She's jus' homesick."

The deputies went away and left us alone. I heard them lock a solid steel door at the other end of the hallway, and immediately I pressed to the side of the bars and tried to look into Violet's cell. Her bed was just out of view, and I could see nothing.

"Violet. Violet," I called in a low voice. After what seemed an eternity, she answered.

"What have they done to you, Violet? Did those bastards beat you up too?"

I heard her whimper and begin to cry.

"Tell me, Violet, did they beat you up?"

"No," she sobbed, "they didn't beat me up." After another long pause she cried out hysterically, "They raped me!"

"They what!"

"They raped me!"

"Of all the godforsaken atrocities!" I heard myself saying, and through me ran bitter hatred. "Are you telling me the truth, Violet? Did those sonofabitches actually do that?"

"Yes, they did!" she screamed. "Now will you shut up!"

"Oh God," I moaned, gripping a bar with my left hand and pressing my head against my swollen wrist. I felt the pain, but I did not care. In my heart was a different kind of pain, a kind that urged me to take a gun or even a knife and kill every lawman in the counties of Pope and Yell. *What in the name of creation have we fallen into?* I asked myself, but the answer was only too plain.

"Violet," I heard myself calling again.

"What?"

"They'll pay for this, Violet. They'll pay well."

She was crying again. "If we'd gone on north like I wanted to we wouldn't be in this mess."

I turned from the bars and looked at the place I was in. It was a large enclosure with several iron bunks along the walls. It was a barred cage with a space between it and the outer walls and windows. In the center of the cage was a metal table with benches on either side. The table and benches were bolted to the concrete floor. *Why have they brought me from Dardanelle and locked me up next to her?* I wondered. *I remember them saying something about a place called Danville, but why have they changed their minds?* I rubbed my swollen wrists and climbed up on the metal table and sat with my feet on a bench. "What a predicament," I said aloud, and heard Violet speak.

"What did you say, Violet?" I moved as quickly as I could back to the barred door.

"I just said I'm sorry, honey. I'm terribly sorry."

"You don't have to be sorry, Violet. You haven't done anything. I'm the one who wouldn't listen."

"But that's not what I'm sorry about," she sobbed.

"Tell me, Violet, what is it?"

"I'm sorry about those brutes and what happened." She again became hysterical and screamed at me. "That's the first time I ever had anyone force me to do a thing like that in my whole life!"

"They'll pay, Violet. They'll pay." I tried to encourage her, but it was no use. She was screaming at me and at them and her words were mostly incoherent and made little sense. Finally a key turned in the metal door at the end of the hallway, and a Russellville deputy stepped into view.

"Y'all better quieten it down up heah 'r yer both gonna have some more comp'ny." He walked to the door of my cell and lowered his voice. "Y'all gotta visitor, boy, an' y'all better not say nothin' 'bout anythang. You know what ah mean." He looked warningly at me and walked back down the hallway. A moment later the steel door opened again and Ma came in.

"Right down theah," the deputy said, pointing in the direction of our cells.

"Ah know wheah it is," the old lady scoffed. "Ah been up heah more times then y'all have." She dismissed the deputy with obvious scorn and approached my cell. She stopped when she came to Violet's, however, and looked in.

"Lordy, chil', whatever happened to you an' yer clothes!" She glanced at me. "You don't need to tell me what happened to you. Ah know." She came to the barred door and lowered her voice. "They kilt my boy in this very buildin' an' they sent my man to Cummins fer life. Thet was 'way back in the late thirties an' he been down theah ever since. An' they'll kill you too, boy, if you don't watch out. They'll kill ya jus' as shore as God made little green apples." Her sad old eyes looked deeply into mine as she remembered. I lowered my eyes and looked at her face and was conscious of gray hair growing around her mouth. I noticed her two teeth, long and yellow, set in gums eaten away by pyorrhea. Her hair, almost a silvery white, was swept back along the sides of her head and knotted in an imperfect bun at the back. "Ah'll try to he'p ya, boy, but they ain't much a poor ol' soul like me can do. It's all a machine an' a c'rrupt 'ministration from Guv'ner McWhitney's office on down."

"What about the federal offices in Little Rock?" I asked hopefully.

"Ain't no use, boy. Ain't no use atall. They won't do a thang. Arkansas claims to have states' rights an' all thet junk an' the United States guv'ment won't butt in."

"The federal will have to take some part in this. That car we were driving was brought across nineteen state lines, and that comes under the Dyer Act."

The old woman shook her head. "They don't care 'bout no D'ar Act 'r whatever it is. They ain't gonna say nothin' 'bout thet car 'r anythang else y'all got thet's any good."

"What about an attorney? Can't he do something about all this?"

"They ain't no 'torney gonna do nothin' fer no one 'round heah. Even if ya had one, he'd jus' be one o' them an' y'all couldn't tell no dif'rence." She glanced at the cell Violet was in and lowered her voice even more. "Ah thank maybe ah'n get her out to the state hospital, but yer gonna hafta do time. They ain't no two ways 'bout thet. You'd jus' as well gentle down an' make the bes' o' it."

"Why did they bring me from Yell County over here? First they had mentioned some place called Danville."

She puckered her mouth warningly and jabbed a gnarled forefinger at the peeled wall. She toned her voice to barely a whisper, spacing each word. "They wanta lis'en an' heah what you two done an' what ya might be gonna do." She shook her head from side to side. "Don't say nothin' thet y'all don't care fer them heahin'."

"I've got the message," I mumbled. Then in a voice as normal as my injured jaw would permit, I asked, "Is Danville someplace near here?"

"Danville's one o' the two seats o' Yell County. Dardanelle is the other."

"Can you get a message to our folks and let them know what is happening?" I had again lowered my voice, but I now lowered it even more. "Not that I expect them to do anything for us. My people are too preachified, and Violet's sister is too stupid."

The old lady rummaged in a dirty purse and took out a pencil and paper. Laboriously she wrote down the words as I spelled them out for her. She then moved to Violet's cell and spoke to her.

"They ain't nobody else gonna bother ya, chil'. They gonna leave ya alone, an' they ain't gonna beat on yer man no more. Y'all ain't nothin' but two mixed-up kiddies an' ah ain't gonna see them do y'all no such way."

I wanted to hug the old lady, but the bars were in my way. Instead I offered my left hand and she took it in both of hers. A mischievous sparkle came into her eyes as she looked into mine. "Now if you ain't a sight, yer teeth knocked out 'n all." She leaned forward. "Ah'd leave ya a good drank o' bonded whiskey but they'd know it right off. Them devils can smell a rat fer a country mile." She glanced behind her at the steel door. "Ah got some pills though. They're called yeller jackets. Take two o' them when yer hurtin' right bad an' they'll stop it." She gave some to me, and she gave some to Violet. She then went to the solid steel door and hammered upon it with her fist. "Le'me out'n this gal-durn place, will ya!"

CHAPTER VII

THE deputy who brought the food to Violet and me was the same one I had seen earlier downstairs at the desk. Without a word he slid tin plates with boiled potatoes and carrots beneath our doors. He then took from under his arm a brown paper bag that was folded down at the end and looked like a package.

"Thet ol' woman left y'all these." He handed a carton of cigarettes to me and pushed a box of bubble gum into Violet's cell. He was about to leave when I spoke to him.

"Will you get me a pencil and a few pieces of paper?"

He looked at me for a moment, then asked, "What y'all want pencil an' paper fer?"

"A writ," I said. "I want to write out a writ and demand that I be taken before a judge and a bond set. I want formal charges filed against me and I want a preliminary hearing. I demand these rights, or my release."

The deputy grinned. "Y'all ain't got no rights, boy. Yer guilty o' givin' thet man over theah a hot check, an' we gonna sen' ya back to Dardanelle an' they gonna give you a fair trial an' sen' ya to Cummins." He rocked back and forth on the balls of his feet. He punched his right fist into the palm of his left hand, and continued. "Yep, they gonna sen' ya to Cummins wheah Cap'n Jones is. An' le'me tell ya somepin' 'bout Cap'n Jones. Thet man gotta long hide. He gotta hide 'bout fi' feet long if it's a n'inch. It gotta silver dollar embedded in one end, an' he'n take thet hide an' jerk a brick out'n the corner o' a buildin'. An' he gonna teach you somepin', boy. He gonna teach you somepin' they ain't no writ 'round heah gonna learn ya."

I swallowed. "What about her?"

"You ain't got no worry 'bout her, boy. We don't sen' much women to Cummins. We gonna take her down to the state hospital soon's she done eatin'. Papers all signed an' ever'thang. We gonna put 'er down theah wheah when she acts up they'n give 'er the shock box." He looked at Violet and said sneeringly, "Y'all jus' chew yer bubble gum, girl, an'— heah, ah'll open this mean ol' door so's you can visit right special with yer boy frien'." He unlocked the door of her cell and left, locking the heavy steel door on his way out.

Immediately Violet came from her cell and stood at my barred door. She reached between the bars and ran one hand up and along one side of my bandaged head. Her eyes no longer glistened like new tar. Now they were frightened and tired eyes, and even haunted. I saw that her hair, once so neatly pinned up and groomed, was untidy and stringy and that the white blouse she wore was soiled and torn. I could not look at her. Instead I lowered my head and looked at her hands on the metal bars. I noticed that blue veins ran along the tops of them and around the sides between thumb and forefinger.

"Honey," she said, forcing my eyes to meet her own.

"Yes?"

"What is it like down at Little Rock where they're taking me?"

"I don't know."

"Is it a hospital or something?"

"That character who was up here said as much."

"B-but I'm not ill, am I, honey? I haven't just imagined all this?"

"You haven't just imagined all this, that's for certain."

"But—but, how long will I have to stay there?"

I looked again at her hands and absently studied the blue veins. "I don't know, Violet. I simply do not know. In a civilized land, maybe not long—if at all. But here in Arkansas, after what we've been through so far, I'm ready to believe anything can happen. You must try to be brave and not fight too hard."

"You mean accept all this?"

"No, not really. But one thing you must understand. What's happening now is the price you have to pay for loving me and going along with my way of life. Even though you aren't guilty of anything, you still have to pay— like everyone else who's ever had anything to do with me. There's some kind of law, beyond this farce of man-made laws, that seems to regulate things. I don't know much about that law, but I believe it exists. And that's the law we've broken."

"Then you do believe in God!"

"Maybe I do. Maybe I don't. Call it god, call it spirit, or call it plain common horse sense. Whatever it is, I guess we all believe in something."

"You mean like the moon out there and what you were saying about believing there's a man in it?"

"I guess."

For several moments she remained silent. "You seem so different now," she said finally. "You don't even talk the same."

"That's because I *am* different, Violet. The man you saw in me outside this jail was a more frightened individual than I'll ever think about being, locked up, even under circumstances such as these."

"Am I different?"

"Not much. You haven't been forced to change. You've only needed to adjust to a new situation. Women are funny that way."

"Are you afraid now?"

"No, not really. But I'm uncomfortable as all get out."

"Then I'm not afraid."

When I didn't say anything, she continued. "Do you want to see me again after we're free?"

"If you can wait that long. Most women can't."

"I can."

I stepped back from the bars and looked into her eyes. "You can write to me at the state prison. I'll write to you up there, and even in Pennsylvania when you get out and go back."

She lowered her eyes. "I don't think I'm going back to Pennsylvania, but wherever I go I'll write."

I started to speak and to say the one thing that I knew she most wanted to hear. I knew, however, that if I said it I would be telling another lie. In our final moments together, I wanted to spare her at least that.

The deputies came late and took Violet out. There were two of them, and they cuffed her hands and pushed her ahead to the steel door. Before she passed through, I saw her look back at me and smile. *Perhaps,* I said to myself, *she'll be wearing that smile when they buckle her down on the shock table at the state hospital.* I bent and picked up the tin plate of boiled potatoes and carrots. I took a small bite of them and threw the disgusting mess out into the corridor between my steel cage and the filthy window.

CHAPTER VIII

I LINGERED on in the cell in Russellville, and it was not until the morning of October twenty-six that they came for me. Again there were four—the sheriff and his three deputies from Yell County. First they opened the cell door and cuffed my hands in front of me. Next they locked a cuff with a long chain to my right ankle. Then a deputy picked up the chain and held it firmly in his left hand, and they pushed me before them past the steel door to the stairway. As we approached the desk, the Russellville deputy sneered at me.

"How y'all thank yer gonna come?"

"I'm not going to attempt anything," I tried to assure him, but I saw by the looks on their faces that he was referring to something else. The sheriff enlightened me.

"He means do y'all thank yer gonna come clean, 'r do y'all thank they'll find ya?"

I still wasn't sure. "Do you mean at court, this morning over at Dardanelle, do I think I'll be convicted?"

"Thet's what he said," the sheriff nodded sarcastically.

I looked at the Russellville deputy. "Yes, I believe I'll be convicted. I really don't see why there should be much fanfare about it. I wrote the check. I've admitted as much. I expect to be sentenced to state prison. All I can see that remains to be done is to determine the amount of time. At any rate, I've already been judged guilty, so what's the big hassle?"

The Yell County sheriff moved closer to me. I expected him to hit me again and I hoped that he wouldn't. As I stood there that morning I was well on my way to recovery from the beating they had previously given me, and I had no desire to go through another bandage routine.

"Le's get this smart bastard out'n heah. He don't even make good sense."

"Air you gonna stop an' talk to Jim?" a deputy asked.

"Ah don't know. Ah'm shore they gonna try 'em this mornin'." The sheriff absently rubbed his chin. He said nothing as he drove toward Dardanelle, but once we had reached the creosote bridge and the car rumbled down on the other side, he spoke to his deputies. "Ah reckon ah better stop an' see what Jim got up his sleeve." He swung the car to a side road and into an unfenced yard that was dirty and littered with tin cans. Chickens squawked and flew everywhere, and ragged children scooted swiftly from the caved-in front porch and hid themselves behind trees and house corners. The sheriff again rubbed his chin. "Jim might not be heah."

"Toot yer horn," one of the deputies beside me suggested. "Maybe you'n rouse 'em thet way."

The sheriff leaned on the car horn. It was a long steady blast that echoed against the dirty brick house and then repeated itself many times as it faded away in the river bottoms. A small girl of perhaps eight ventured from behind an oak tree and crept forward.

"Yer daddy home?" the sheriff called to her.

"He an' mamma still sleepin'."

One of the deputies laughed. "Ol' Jim got ten already an' still tryin' fer more!"

The front door opened and a red-headed, tousle-haired man looked out at the automobile. He blinked his eyes and squinted into the bright morning.

The sheriff motioned him over. "C'mon out, Jim. Ah gotta talk to ya 'bout the trial."

The man left the porch and approached the car. He was dressed in a filthy blue bathrobe that was pulled together and tied at the waist with a strand of binder twine. He was barefoot, and his feet were slender and crusted with dirt at the heel and between each toe.

"Wail, ah'll be durn," he said, peering into the automobile and recognizing its occupants. "How y'all been?" He reared back and extended his hand. "Sheriff, ah ain't seen you in a coon's age!" His gaze traveled back and settled upon me cuffed between the two deputies. "Is this the one ah heared 'bout?"

"Thet's 'em. When air ya plannin' to persecute?"

"Wail now," the prosecutor answered, "ah reckon ah'n get over this mornin'." After a pause he added, "Y'all takin' 'em on over now, ain't ya?"

"Straight as a crow flies," the sheriff assured him.

The prosecutor thought for a moment. He raked a toe in the dust of the yard and kicked at a chicken. Several children eased closer. "Somebody'll hafta go down to the Bucket o' Blood an' roust out Jedge Haight."

One of the deputies beside me spoke. "He was up to Fanny Lou's place this mornin'."

The sheriff chuckled. "Thet's more'n likely wheah we'll find 'em now. He shore do like them gals up theah."

"Who don't!" said the prosecutor. "Thet Jeanie Mae's sproutin' out'n front like a young heifer."

The men guffawed.

"Ah heared she jus' quit school altogether," the sheriff commented.

One of the deputies butted in. "Hell, she done know more'n the teacher do already!"

The men laughed again, then the sheriff said seriously, "Look, Jim, we'll go by an' pick up Jedge Haight an' you'n come on over. We'll meet ya at the courthouse an' get this trial under way."

Somewhere inside the house a child screamed. Moments later, after some great commotion, a woman with a broom came fighting a rooster through the front door. The prosecutor looked absently at her, then back at the sheriff. "How ya thank he gonna come?"

The sheriff seemed surprised at the question. "Hell, how do ah know! Yer the persecutor. Whyn't ya ask 'em?"

"Awright, ah'll do thet." He stuck his head through the open window and looked at me. "How y'all thank yer gonna come, boy?"

I cleared my throat. "Under the circumstances, it's hard to say. Some appeals court beyond the state of Arkansas could well turn me loose."

"He's a smart sonofabitch," the sheriff said. "We took some out'n 'em, but they's plenty left. We gonna go easy on 'em though. We wanta leave 'em good an' healthy fer Cummins Farm." He winked at the prosecutor. "Cap'n Jones an' them cotton an' pea rows'll take some o' thet piss an' vinegar out'n 'em."

They all laughed.

"Awright then," said the red-headed prosecutor, "y'all go by an' get Jedge Haight an' ah'll get on some clothes an' meet ya over theah. Won't take long to find 'em one way 'r t'other." He kicked at another chicken.

The sheriff pulled the car from the littered yard. "We gotta fin' Jedge Haight an' get 'em over to the courthouse 'fore he gets too stinkoed." He stepped on the gas pedal and the automobile roared through the small town of Dardanelle.

The whiskered man who came to the car was on crutches. The left leg of his blue denim overalls was pulled up under a stump and pinned somewhere in back. As he walked toward us from the house called "Fanny Lou's place," a girl of twelve or thirteen walked beside him and helped hold him up. The judge was obviously already half drunk.

"Y'all thank you'n make it over to the courthouse to try this case?"

The judge looked at the sheriff through blurred eyes. "Don't know why not," he said. Then, "How y'all thank yer gonna come, boy?"

"It all depends, Your Honor. If I can have a lawyer and you will listen to my side of the story, maybe I can get a fair sentence."

The sheriff spoke. "This smart bastard gonna take whatever sentence you give 'em, Jedge, an' he gonna like it."

"Now jus' a minute," the judge said. "If he got somepin' to say, let 'em say it. Thet's a man's rights."

"Oh, he'n talk if he wants to," the sheriff conceded.

The judge shuffled his weight on his crutches. "Air ya guilty, boy, 'r ain't ya?"

The sheriff looked quickly at the bleary-eyed judge. "Now jus' a goddamn minute," he objected. "Air we gonna have this trial heah 'r over to the courthouse? They's a lotta people waitin' over theah who air jus' as anxious to know 'bout thet as you air."

"Ah was jus' askin'," the judge hedged.

"Wail, don't ask. We come by an' talked to Jim. He's gonna meet us over theah to persecute—y'all wanta squeeze in heah with us an' go on over?"

The judge looked at an old Ford parked nearby. "Naw. Jeanie Mae'n he'p me over. She drives purty good."

"Awright," the sheriff said, "le's get on over an' start the trial."

The citizens gathered in the well-polished courtroom were wearing their Sunday best. Some of the faces were stern, but most were curious. There were women wearing bonnets and seated on wooden benches near the front of the room, and there were men in blue overalls and white shirts standing in doorways and seated farther back. A few of the people had lunches, and I imagined that many of those present had walked for miles out of the river bottom country. The deputies, now pretentious and officiously correct, pushed me past the spectators. They pushed me in front of the bench and to a table with two chairs. The deputy who held the chain to my right ankle indicated the chair on the left, and I sat down. He took the other one, and the place became quiet. I looked around, but the deputy beside me told me to look straight ahead and to be still. Even so, I noticed the flags above the huge leather chair that the judge would occupy. The one on top was the flag of my country, a symbol of my guarantee of equal and fair justice at any time. The one below it and slightly to the right was the flag of Arkansas. Somehow, it overshadowed the national flag and made it seem small and very unimportant.

Everywhere behind me now the people talked. Their

voices were low, almost religious in tone, and the question the voices asked most frequently was, "Do ya thank he'll come clean, 'r do ya thank they'll find 'em?"

"Stan' up," the deputy beside me commanded. As I did, the judge came through a door to one side of the bench. He worked his way up to the huge leather chair and sat down. The girl stood beside him and took the crutches the judge handed her. The deputy prodded me with his elbow. "Set down," he commanded, and the judge picked up a ballpeen hammer and struck a wooden block three times. Court was in session.

"Whata y'all got the prisoner charged with?"

The prosecutor, now dressed in suntan trousers and a faded yellow shirt, spoke from the side of the courtroom. "He give Diamond Cutter's Jewelry Store a bad check fer fi' thousan' dollars."

"Anybody got the check?" the judge asked.

The prosecutor shifted uneasily. "The man at the store won't let us have it. He said he don't want to persecute nobody long as he got his diamonds back."

Behind me the sheriff spoke. "We gonna persecute anyways, Jedge. The State o' Arkansas can do thet."

"Ah know the law, sheriff." The judge seemed angered. "Y'all jus' le'me take care o' the law. You'n take care o' the prisoner."

Someone laughed.

"Ah'll have no disorder in this courtroom," the judge said sternly, striking the wooden block with the ballpeen hammer. Then to me, "Air y'all guilty 'r not guilty, boy?"

The sheriff interrupted. "Why'nt hell you wanta ask 'em thet fer? He done said he was. All you gotta do is give 'em twenty years an' we'n call the truck from Cummins Farm to come get 'em."

The judge looked at the sheriff for a long moment. "This court gotta make findin's. Now, air ya guilty, boy, 'r ain't ya?"

I started to stand and address the court, but the deputy pulled me back. "Maybe I could have a lawyer, Your Honor. He could help me figure out the best course to take under these circumstances."

The judge looked around the courtroom. "Ain't no lawyer heah right now, lessen y'all want Jim to take yer side too."

"Ah'n be his lawyer," the sheriff offered. "Ah'n talk fer his side jus' as good as the persecutor can."

"You ain't no lawyer, though," the prosecutor objected.

The sheriff laughed. "Ah'm as gooder one as you air, Jim."

"Awright, you'n be his lawyer, sheriff. Now, ah'm gonna read what he's charged with an' y'all thank 'bout it ... on October sixteen he went over heah to Diamond Cutter's Jewelry Store an' give thet man a bad check fer fi' thousan' dollars. Thet's forg'ry, an' thet's utterin'. He'n be sentenced on both counts."

The sheriff pulled a chair up beside mine. "Ah wanta talk to 'em a minute, Jedge. Looky, boy, ah'm yer lawyer now. Jus' ferget ah'm also county sheriff. If you plead guilty, the jedge gonna give ya a straight sentence. If he hafta call up a jury from back theah, they gonna go rough on ya. These people in Yell air all good Baptist people, an' they gonna see thet y'all get what's comin' to ya. Heah, ah'll show ya in the law book what it says." He looked around. "Somebody gotta penal book 'round heah?"

"Take this'n to 'em," the judge said, and the young girl walked down from behind the bench and to the table. She handed the book to the sheriff and giggled.

"You'n go back now, Jeanie Mae," the sheriff said. Then to me, "Looky heah, boy. Fer forg'ry you'n get ten years. Fer the utterin' part you'n get another ten. Thet's twenty years strung out. Now, if you plead guilty an' don't cause no trouble, ah'll tell the jedge to give ya fi' on each one an' run 'em together. Whata y'all say?"

The prosecutor objected. "The lawyer can't tell the prisoner what he gonna get."

"The hell ah can't!" the sheriff exploded. "You jus' persecute this case. Ah'll offend it." He picked up the code book and threw it at the tousle-haired man. The book hit the wall near the prosecutor's head and flopped crazily into the midst of a group of spectators. The book reminded me of the squawking rooster I had seen the woman at the prosecutor's house chase through the front door. "Durn you anyhow," the sheriff sputtered.

The judge rapped the block with the hammer. "Y'all gotta settle down a mite 'r ah'll 'journ this trial 'til ya cool off."

"It ain't me causin' no trouble," the prosecutor argued. "Heck, ah ain't mad 'bout nothin'."

"It were you tellin' me what ah can do an' what ah can't," the sheriff protested. "Yer jus' tryin' to crawfish now, Jim. Ah know yer game."

"Y'all better settle down. Ah'm warnin' ya Ah'm gonna 'journ this trial."

"Your Honor—" I began, but the deputy prodded my ribs with his elbow.

"Jus' keep quiet," he warned. "When the jedge wants ya he knows wheah ya air."

"Let 'em say somepin'," the judge ruled.

"Your Honor, I'd like to be permitted to stand up and state my case, since I'm the one on trial here."

"Let 'em stan' up," the judge ordered. He turned to the girl and whispered something, and she left the courtroom.

"To begin with, Your Honor, I was beaten up here in jail

for no reason at all. Violet, the woman I was arrested with, was raped and brutally treated."

The sheriff jumped to his feet. "You got whupped 'cause you tried to make a break from us, boy. An' what they done over in Pope County ain't got nothin' to do with us heah."

The judge agreed. "Yer lawyer's right, boy. What they done over theah ain't no consarn o' ourn. Now, finish yer case so's ah'n get on with the sentencin'."

"Well, even so," I continued, "I don't believe I'm being fairly treated. The man I'm accused of giving the check to isn't even present. The check isn't here. I'm being forced to say things I don't want to say. What kind of justice is that?"

The judge looked down at me for a few moments. Presently the girl returned to the bench and handed him a brown paper bag. The judge swiveled around in the huge leather chair and sat for a time with his back to the courtroom. Finally he turned back and smacked his lips. He continued to observe me for several more moments.

"We gonna treat you fair, boy. We gonna treat you jus' as fair an' square as the days is long. Yer charged heah with two counts o' breakin' the law—forg'ry an' utterin'. Now, how air ya gonna plead?"

"Ah'm pleadin' 'em guilty," the sheriff said.

"Awright, this court fin's ya guilty by yer own omission. Fer the forg'ry, ah'm sentencin' ya to three years at hard labor on Cummins Prison Farm. Fer the utterin', ah'm—"

"Ah object to thet, Jedge." The prosecutor pushed forward. "The people want 'em to have more time. Thet ain't enough, an' we ain't a-gonna stan' fer it."

"Ah'm his lawyer, Jedge, an' ah say give 'em fi' years on each count an' run 'em together. Thet way he'n do fi' years an' get out, if they don't kill 'em 'fore then."

The prosecutor started to speak, but the sheriff stared him down. Instead the prosecutor fumbled at a button on his faded yellow shirt and looked at the floor.

"Wail, Jim, whata y'all gotta say about thet?"

The prosecutor looked uneasily at the citizens behind him. "Ah guess if thet's what y'all gonna do it's awright. He prob'ly should have twenty, though."

"Awright then," the judge decided, "fi' years on each count." He looked at the courtroom and struck the wooden block with the ballpeen hammer. "Be it known heah in the great State o' Arkansas thet a prisoner has been foun' guilty by his own omission o' forg'ry an' utterin'. Be it further known thet this honorable court passes jedgment on thet prisoner at this time. Mark thet down on the book theah, Jeanie Mae. It is the order o' this court thet this prisoner be sent down to Cummins Prison Farm fer fi' years fer forg'ry an' another fi' years fer utterin'. He'n sarve both these sentences together, but he gotta do hard labor—an' may the good Lord have mercy 'pon his poor soul. Court a'journed."

When the judge brought down the hammer and announced that court was adjourned, pandemonium broke out in the back of the courtroom. "They found 'em," a man yelled out a window. "Go tell Ben at the feed store. He said he wanted to know soon's it happened." People moved right and left and crowded in. Somewhere behind me a woman sobbed. "Ah always jus' cry when nobody don't come clean." And another woman, "Ah thank we oughta have special services in church fer thet boy an' pray it out." The deputy nudged me. "Awright, boy. We'n go now." As we went through the doorway, a small boy ran by and I heard him yell, "They foun' 'em guilty as the dickens." And down at the automobile, a woman pressed forward and offered her hand. Her palm was soft and she squeezed my hand meaningfully. "Ah jus' wanta hol' yer han' an' ask you to take yer medicine like a man." The sheriff intervened. "He ain't got no time fer thet now. We gotta rush 'em on up to Danville to jail."

The sheriff turned the car from the courthouse and down through the center of town. On the narrow street, people lined the boardwalk and pressed against the hitching rails on either side. As we passed the jewelry store, I saw the anemic-looking little man standing outside. Why, I wondered, had the man I had swindled not been at my trial. Somewhere on the edge of town, as the automobile pulled onto State Road 27, the word *justice* came to my mind. I thought of Ma and the evening Violet and I had come to Dardanelle. I remembered the taxi drivers and the angry crowd who had fenced me in on the sidewalk at the hotel. I thought of the beating that the deputies had given me, and I thought of Violet and her sad plight with the law at Russellville. Words kept ringing in my ears.

"If we'd gone on north like I wanted to we wouldn't be in this mess."

"Awright then, fi' years on each count."

I thought of the national flag that adorned the wall in the ancient courtroom, and I thought of the Arkansas flag and my recent experience. And then I could hold it no longer. I lowered my head to my handcuffed wrists and cried silently all the way into Danville.

CHAPTER IX

THE Danville jail was a mass of steel erected on the second floor of a house. I soon learned that the jailer and his wife and children occupied the lower level, and that a heavy steel door separated their living quarters from the small rectangle which led to the stairway, winding to the left and up to a landing and a simple barred door of the lockup. I was the only prisoner, and my first evening there the jailer's wife came up the stairs and cautiously slid a plate of food beneath the bars and turned to go. Below her, at the foot of the stairway, several children pushed forward and stared up curiously.

"He's up theah," I heard one say. And from another, "Gosh, he got fi' yeahs. When he gets out ah'll be fifteen!"

"You kids get back in theah," the woman screamed, and a few moments later she closed the heavy steel door and the place became quiet.

I looked at the plate of food on the floor and couldn't believe my eyes. There were chunks of hot buttered cornbread, a mountain of pinto beans with ham hocks, and a quart of buttermilk. I picked up the food and walked to the only window. I set the milk on the sill and, standing, began to eat. Absently I noticed that beyond the window alongside the house was a cabbage patch. Off to the right by the dirt road was an oak tree, and farther away there were cotton fields. I ate slowly, and contentedly. Although there was more food than I could ever eat in one meal, I pushed the beans around in my mouth to make them last and savored the delicious meat of the ham hocks. Then the heavy steel door opened and the jailer came up the stairway.

"The people heah in Danville wanta sang ya some songs," he announced. "Ah want ya to go to the winder an' look inter'sted. These folks air all good solid pillers o' Danville society. Ah want ya to make 'em feel wonderful."

"Sure," I said, thankful for the pinto beans and the cornbread and rich buttermilk. I was also very much aware of what might happen to me should I fail to comply. I walked to the window and looked out upon the empty cabbage patch. "When are they coming?" I started to inquire, but the jailer scowled.

"You don't worry none 'bout thet. You jus' stan' an' wait. They'll be heah."

And they were. From around the corner of the building and into the cabbage patch marched the cream of Danville society. There were tall vested men with guitars strapped over their shoulders. There were bonneted women with hymnals. There were young boys and giggling girls and dirty-faced children, and dogs and cats and one lean pig of the bacon variety. As the line filed up and formed into ranks, the people sang: *"Le's all march together fer a prisoner o' the Lord. . . ."* And their eyes lifted up and looked at my window and the voices continued. "He's Working for

Satan"—"There's Sin in the Valley"—"Judgment Day"—on and on they sang, past twilight and into the night. Automobiles pulled up and gave light, and the men with the guitars ran their fingers expertly over the frets. *"Lord, I've drifted far from home . . ."*—and at one point a woman, overcome by the words of a song they were singing, ran to the edge of the cabbage patch and shook her fist at my window. "If y'all don't mend yer wicked ways yer bound fer hell!" she screamed. The children took her words as a signal and pelted my window with clods from the cabbage patch and any rocks they could find.

"Le's try thet prisoner-o'-the-Lord song ag'in. My daddy use to sang thet all the time an' ah jus' love it."

"Can y'all get thet in F? Thet key we was playin' in is jus' too low fer good sangin'."

When the people filed away, the children stayed. They stayed and threw rocks and clods, and as the time passed the children grew braver and threw the cabbages instead. And the cabbages splattered against the side of the building, and the voices called from across the cotton fields, and one by one the children disappeared into the black night. "Hanni-bal-l-l . . . Alexan-der-r-r . . . y'all better get yerselves home . . . it's nigh on bedtime. . . ."

The next morning I rubbed the calves of my legs and looked out the window at the place where the people had sung. The cabbages were bruised and many were uprooted, and wilted cabbage leaves formed a green pad in the middles and furrows of the patch. When the jailer came to my cell I ventured what I thought might be a polite gesture.

"That was sure kind of the Danville people to take time to come to my window and sing songs to me."

"You dirty devil," he growled. "Look at my cabbage patch. If it hadn't been fer you, all this wouldn't o' happened."

By the time the prison truck arrived at Danville from Cummins Farm, I had given up any hope of breaking jail. Handcuffed and shackled, I followed the jailer down the stairway and out past the people gathered near the front door. On my way to the truck, I noticed a dark-headed man standing to one side with a .45 strapped to his waist. The man wore suntans, and shifted his eyes, but every moment watched another man he referred to as "Cap'n Reed."

"Y'all jus' get right up in theah an' get ya a nice soft place on thet ol' wooden bench an' don't give us no-o-o trouble."

It was the dark-headed man who addressed me, but once the captain had disappeared into the jail building, he approached the cage I was sitting in and spoke to me in a different voice. "Heck, ah don't want ya to thank thet ah thank ah'm big ner nothin'. Ah'm jus' a convict doin' time like you air. Ah jus' got my duty." He glanced uneasily toward the jail building. "Y'all got a cigarette on ya?"

I handed him a cigarette through the wire mesh and watched him back away. "You mean you're serving a sentence in prison and you carry a gun?"

"Shore," he said, keeping an eye on the jailhouse door. "Ah ain't even s'pose to be talkin' to y'all like this. But heck, ah don't care, long as Cap'n Reed don't see me."

"I hear it's pretty rough at Cummins," I said. "They beat convicts up with a strap, don't they?"

"It ain't too bad, if ya pull yer own time an' let other guys do thern. They might put ya out trusty after yer theah a while. Never can tell. Thet's what ah am, a trusty. Heck, ah'm jus' like you 'r anybody else."

Captain Reed came out of the building carrying a sheaf of papers. The dark-headed man again changed his voice.

"Now this .45 ya see on my hip is loaded. If you give Cap'n Reed the leas' bit o' trouble, ah'll turn right aroun' through the cab winder an' shoot yer goddamn butt off. Got thet?"

"Yes sir," I answered.

"Y'all don't hafta *sir* me. Ah'm jus' a convict like you air. But y'all better say 'sir' to Cap'n Reed, an' y'all better be lookin' at the groun' at his feet when you say it. Got thet?"

"You better believe it," I answered sharply.

The trusty looked doubtfully at me but said nothing more. He went to the cab of the truck and climbed in, and the truck moved out. As the white line of the highway began to unroll behind us, I thought of the many things that had come to pass in the very few days I had been in Arkansas.

They're not sending me up the river, I said to myself. *They're taking me down—a hundred and fifty miles to the southeast!*

The white line raced to one side as the truck sped past a loaded cotton wagon. And before long my thoughts turned to my future and what it held, and that lasted me all the way to the huge gate of the Arkansas State Penitentiary.

CHAPTER X

GOVERNOR, oh Governor, I am confused. In your penal system you have less than a dozen hired employees. As I understand it, you have a Board of Pardons, Paroles and Probation. You have six men serving on this board, with a chairman or director acting as top dog.

Next come the wardens, large and small, with Captain Jones serving as superintendent of Cummins and Tucker prison farms. At Cummins you have a field captain—or little warden—for each of your four prison camps. Is it true that convict trusties *run* the Arkansas State Penitentiary?

I am surprised. I had expected a walled prison with paid guards overseeing the inmates. I am surprised that convict guards carry guns and issue orders to the very men they are confined with. I am also surprised that instead of high walls you have mile after mile of fertile land. How do you do it? How do you keep the convict guards from running away? How do you keep the men in blue from wandering off, through the tall corn to the cotton fields and across the levee to the wooded lands along the Arkansas River?

Your convict guards are plenty rough. They act mean, they talk mean, and they are mean. They beat and stomp and kick and shoot and, for some strange reason, seem only to know one compound word—relating to mothers.

But you've got me now, so I'll be good. I'll be as good as anyone could reasonably expect under the circumstances. What is that you say? You don't care if I'm good or bad so long as I pick a ton of cotton each day! What about my re-habilitation? Oh, your penal system isn't based on that? You just make life such a miserable hell for your convicts that none would ever dare violate your sacred codes again. But I see men who have come back—some for a second, a third and even a fourth term. They are your favorite sons, you say? How right you are!

They are the cream of your Arkansas crop, your trusties, out of the hills after raping their mothers, their sons and their poor old fathers' heifer calves. They carry your guns and they fink and they snitch and they tell shaky stories which show them always in a favorable light.

But what of your out-of-staters? They know that if you didn't kill them the first time around you surely will the next. Thus your neighboring states catch the brunt of your hell-fire-and-brimstone philosophy. Half-dead men, crippled and maimed and nearly insane, stumble across your state lines and into receiving wards across the nation. These men are not your favorite sons. They do not carry your guns. They fight you, at least in spirit, every inch of the way. And many are not even guilty. But you make sure that your out-of-staters, although released from Arkansas servitude, continue to serve their sentences until the day they die.

As I look around your prison, I see white clouds pass under

deep blue skies. I see grasshoppers flit by the roadside, and, although it is late in the year, it is still sultry and hot and I see heat waves and dust devils shimmer and dance above and beyond your cotton and pea rows. They are long rows, perhaps without end, and I'm sure that for me you have a very special one.

Governor, oh Governor, I am determined. I am young and healthy and can pick more cotton, gather more peas, strip more sorghum cane—fight harder, think deeper, love longer than any goddamned Arkansan who ever lived.

CHAPTER XI

THE convict trusty who signed me in was a short, rotund fellow with a quiet, unassuming manner. He talked seriously, when he did talk, and quite frequently used words and phrases of a religious nature. We were alone in the receiving room at Camp Number One, and as he fingerprinted me and arranged my commitment papers I questioned him.

"What is it like here at Cummins?"

"Wail," he answered, "they's still hope. Ah can't say too much. Ah'n jus' give ya some good, sound advice. Keep yer mouth shut and do what yer tol', an' other then thet all ah can say is jus' pray an' hope fer the bes'."

"Will I do my time at this camp?"

"Not right off. They ain't no convicts heah yet, 'ceptin' us office workers. It's jus' new. They'll take ya to Seven Camp firs'. It's 'bout two miles on down the road. Later though, ah heah they gonna move all the hard shells up heah. Maybe you'n stay at Seven Camp an' won't hafta come."

"Do they really whip men here, like I've heard?"

"You'll hafta learn 'bout thet as ya go along."

"How's the food?"

He glanced at me. "You'n get by, ah guess."

The door opened and another trusty came in. He was a tall man, in suntans, with a scar across his forehead and down to his left eye. His mouth was large, and he spoke loudly, and upon his face and in his demeanor was a hint of banter.

"Is this the new skinner Cap'n Reed brought in on the meat wagon?" Then to me: "Whata y'all heah fer, boy?"

"For forgery and uttering," I answered, wiping the ink from my fingers.

"You better learn to say better'n thet when Cap'n Burr asks what yer heah fer. You better say: To pick cotton, Cap'n. Ah'm heah to pick all the goddamn cotton on Cummins Prison Farm!" He leaned back and his big mouth flapped as he ha-hahed.

"Awright, Scarface, you'n take 'em now. Ah'm all done." The little fellow turned to me as I left the room. "Good luck now, an' don't ferget to keep prayin'."

The trusty escorted me to the front of the building and out a door. "Wait right heah," he said, and went to one of four concrete guard towers and untied a saddled horse. He mounted and swung the horse around. He waved an arm at a back tower and a guard from that point waved back. Then the trusty motioned me across the shallow ditch that formed the guardline from tower to tower. "Down thet road," he indicated, and followed behind some ten paces. "Them air high-power-rifle men on them towers. Y'all wanta stay well on the shoulder o' the road an' don't get too much off'n the bar ditch. They'll pick ya off shore as shootin'."

I moved closer to the center of the dirt roadway. "They pretty rough on a person down here?" I asked.

"'Pends on who ya air an' how much they down on ya. Take me, now, ah ain't had my butt busted in over two years. Actually, ah ain't big ner nothin', but they ain't down on me. My fall par'ner though, he never did make it out trusty. He gets it 'bout ever' day—sometimes two an' three times. He don't min' it though. He gotta harder ass then this horse ah'm ridin'." He reared back in the saddle and laughed loudly. "Hard Ass they call 'em. Take me, though, ah'll never ferget the firs' time Cap'n Burr got on me. It were the las' time too. 'Get down theah,' he tol' me an' ah got down. Back he went with thet strap an' hit me square in the rear end. 'Oh, oo-oo . . . goddamn . . . geeeezuzzz . . . Cap'n,' ah yelled, an' he started laughin'. Started laughin' so hard thet he couldn't finish an' ah got off with thet one lick. It were the firs' an' the las' an' ah shore as hell don't want no more. Over theah," he directed, and I crossed another guardline and entered the yard of Camp Number Seven. A trusty met me at a side door of the mess hall.

"Ah'm the yardman," he volunteered. "Ah'm in charge o' the whole damn camp an' all you bulls while yer in camp. Ah'm a convict, jus' like you air—on'y ah got pull, lotsa pull. Ah'n have yer butt busted any time ah want, an' ah will too. It's you 'r me, an' buddy, ah ain't losin'." He showed me to one of the two tables that ran the full length of the wooden building. He then called to someone in back. "Get this new skinner somepin' to eat out heah. He's already a month late fer the cotton crop. Hurry it up an' we'n get 'em out on the doby wagon."

A one-eared man wearing a filthy apron came scurrying in from the kitchen. He set a metal tray and a single pot on the planks in front of me. "Tops an' bottoms," he said, and hurried away. Soon he returned with a pan of bread. I examined the scroungy mess. Inside the pot were turnips, whole and unpeeled, cooked in plain water and with tops on. The bread was made of yellow cornmeal without benefit of grease or baking soda. Nevertheless I ate a few bites before pushing the pile of garbage away from me. The one-eared man, who had been standing in the center of the mess hall by a cast iron stove, came forward. "What's the matter? Don't you like my cookin' boy?" He called to the yardman. "Hey, Max, this mammyjammer don't like my cookin'. Y'all oughta have his butt busted."

The yardman seemed irritated. "Look, you one-eared bastard, get them cans on the doby wagon so Scarface can get 'em out to the long line. Thet long line rider's gonna raise some hell if chow's late ag'in today."

The sun bore down with intense heat as I sat in the wagon and guided the two old nags from the camp toward the open field. The tall trusty, armed with a .45, crouched behind me near the back of the wagon bed. "Whup 'em up," he said worriedly. "Thet long line rider's gonna blow his top if we don't get on out."

"Be quitting time before long anyhow, won't it? What time do they knock off?"

The trusty glanced at the sun. "Knock off! We gotta long time to go yet. These people down heah don't know what quittin' time is. They count ya off'n the yard with a flashlight in the mornin's an' back on with one at night. An' in between times yer humpin' an' jumpin'—by the way, wheah y'all from?"

"I was born in Oklahoma."

"Thet ain't too bad. They don't mind no Okies too much down heah. It's them Texas people they can't stan'. They flat after them. Talk too much. Thank ever'thang they got's bigger'n ourn. Ain't nobody bigger'n Cap'n Jones. He's God if they ever was one. We call 'em the Green Hornet—'cause he drives thet green Oldsmobile an' stings hell out'n convicts with thet hide, ah guess. Wheah'd y'all fall from?"

"Dardanelle. Forgery and uttering. Five on each, run together. Is this your home state?"

"Shore 'nough is. Never been out'n Arkansas. Live heah, raised heah, guess ah'll die heah."

"Where did you fall from?"

"Right out'n Little Rock, me'n Ol' Crabtree. You'll meet 'em out heah in the long line. Call 'em Ol' Hard Ass. Anyways, we come down the same time. Got ten years apiece fer burgl'ry. Ah never even hit the long line. Made trusty the same day ah got heah. Been guardin' Ol' Crabtree ever since."

"Why didn't they turn your fall partner out trusty?"

"Aw, he got 'em teed off at 'em when we was in Little Rock. Cussed out the persecutor an' wouldn't plead guilty to charges. Made 'em hafta pay fer a jury trial. Little Rock sent a *message* to Cummins 'bout 'em. Cap'n Jones lis'ens to them messages. Thet's politics down heah. Cap'n Jones knows all they is about politics to ever be knowed."

I looked at the cotton rows we were passing and saw that frost had bitten the leaves and in spots they were turning brown. On each row the cotton was white and piled high, and the rows formed long lines that ran together off to the distance and woodlands. Ahead of us in the open fields I could now see mounted riders and mules and wagons, and figures pulling white sacks. And moments later, I heard the sounds. Piercing screams that chilled my blood and, under the hot sun, made me fearful and cold inside. The screams rose and fell and gurgled and faded away into nothingness across the delta land. Then the screams began all over again, and I turned to the convict trusty behind me and asked weakly, "What are they doing to him?"

"Hell, ah don't know. Could be anythang. Looks like they're givin' 'em the nail treatment. Jus' pushin' a few little ol' needles under his toenails to he'p 'em remember to pay his dues."

"Dues?"

"Shore. Union dues, they call 'em—so's he won't get whupped 'r nothin'."

"Can they do that here? That's not legal—"

"You bes' ferget it. Don't even look thet way 'r they'll have you out theah, wired up long distance on the Tucker telephone. Heah, pull off heah."

I guided the nags off the turnrow and across the bar ditch to the edge of the field as the trusty indicated.

"Is this awright, Stud?" he called to a mounted horseman.

The horseman came over and reined in. Without a word he readjusted himself in the saddle and threw one leg over the saddle horn. For what seemed an eternity he sat and looked with an expression of complete disgust upon his face. He surveyed the nags and, for several moments, focused his gaze upon the bright shiny knob at the top of a harness hame. He looked at the wagon I was sitting in, and I had the feeling that he would only vaguely remember seeing me there. Finally, he straightened himself again in the saddle, nudged his horse to the back of the wagon, and reached low for the trusty's gun. He spun the cylinder and inspected its contents. Then he pulled back the hammer and pushed the muzzle of the gun against the trusty's forehead.

"Scarface, yer late ag'in," he said simply. "This doby wagon's s'pose to be heah at twelve noon an' it's two thirty."

The trusty started to reply but the mounted rider paid no

mind. "You sorry sonofabitch. Ah'm gonna put a nice roun' hole right theah, jus' a little bit under thet scar." He reached down and with a forefinger touched a spot on Scarface's forehead. He weaved back and forth and the gun also weaved in front of the trusty's face. And all that the trusty seemed able to say was, "Ah know, Stud—ah know, Stud—ah'll get it out heah in time from now on."

The mounted rider lowered the gun and, quite unexpectedly, handed it back to the tall man. "Naw, Scarface, ah ain't a-gonna shoot ya. Not now, leastwise." He turned in his saddle and called to a man wearing blues and pulling a cotton sack. "Blue Moon, come get this mammyjammer's gun. He got yer job now."

Blue Moon rushed over and started to reach for the trusty's gun, but two bullets kicked at the dust by a wheel of the wagon. "You shoot him an' ah'll shoot you, an' ah got myself a ninety-day furlough." The voice came from a high-power-rifle man sitting farther back in the field. I then realized that the trusty had stood up in the wagon bed and pointed the .45 at the man who had threatened to kill him. The mounted horseman acted swiftly. He brought his own gun up from its holster and knocked Scarface from the wagon and into the dust of the turnrow. "Blue Moon," the rider said casually, "when this bastard comes to, give 'em a cotton sack an' put 'em in One Spot." Then to the convicts in general he ordered: "Make it up."

Across the field I saw men pull themselves from the straps of cotton sacks and form into squads. Each squad, followed by a man in suntans armed with a shotgun, came to the turnrow and stood waiting. I noticed that five squads made up the long line, and that each squad stood separated from the others by some thirty feet, with a shotgun man some fifteen paces behind each squad. Once they were settled, the mounted horseman rode down the line and counted the men in blue. He did some figuring, fingerwise, and looked at a paper he took from a shirt pocket. Satisfied, he then gave a second order for the men to "fall out" and turned to me.

"Air y'all gonna do yer time sittin' on thet goddamn doby wagon? C'mon—c'mon, new skinner. Le's eat."

"I ate before they brought me out," I started to explain, but the horseman threw his leg over the saddle horn and looked at me. I was aware that the men from the field had seated themselves in two long lines facing each other. I was also aware that the shotgun men had backed off into the fields nearby, and that farther out mounted horsemen with high-power rifles sat and waited. I climbed down from the wagon and started over to join the sitting men.

"Wheah y'all from?" the mounted man asked me.

"I fell out of Yell County—Dardanelle."

"You ain't a Texan, air ya?"

"No," I replied, "I'm a displaced wild Indian from Okie-land."

The rider reared back in his saddle and laughed loudly. He slapped his leg with a black dusty hat. "Y'all heah thet, men? Ah got me a home town boy heah. He's awright. He fell from the same place ah fell from. We gonna name 'em Darda-nelle." He dismounted and came over where I had seated myself with the men from the fields. He squatted down and scratched in the dust of the turnrow. "Hell, ah fell out'n Yell County in 'thirty-one. Killed my ol' lady an' got life. Been down heah ever since."

"Won't they give you a parole?" I asked. "Surely you've been here long enough to deserve that."

"Naw," he said, tracing a figure in the dust. "When ah firs' come heah ah excaped. Ah was ridin' the Tucker long line an' ah took the whole damn bunch with me down into Louisiana—all thet wanted to go, thet is. We killed a shotgun guard thet tried to stop us." He chuckled. "Never ferget, we had one sonofabitch in the long line who had a wooden leg. We knew he'd scream to high mercy—have the law on us 'fore we got across the river. One high-power man started to jus' shoot 'em, but ah thought o' somepin' better. So we took his wooden leg off'n 'em an' stuck it up in the mud. He couldn't get back to camp ner nowheah to tell nothin'." He again laughed loudly and took off his hat. " 'Bout my wife, though, don't ever do like one sonofabitch done. This ol' thang use to draw birthday cards, an' Christmas cards an' what not, an' he use to pass 'em out to anyone who looked like they might be gettin' homesick 'r needin' one. So this ol' thang made one fer me. Never ferget what it said. It said, 'Dear Stud, roses are red, violets are blue. May Jesus look after you, the whole year through.' Now thet's po'try, an' ah ain't so goddamned inhuman thet ah don't like 'r 'preciate po'try. But under thet the sonofabitch said, 'Stud, I seriously hope thet you get a parole sometime, and thet you go join your wife and keep on being a good man.' "

"And you had killed your wife?" I queried.

"Hell, Dardanelle, ah jus' tol' ya ah did. Shot 'er sixteen times right in the gizzard."

"Did you say anything to the fellow?"

"Not much then. Ah was ranked an' carryin' One Spot in the long line an' had a lot o' heat on me. But later on, when ah got out trusty an' started ridin' the long line ag'in, ah stomped his ass ever' day fer about two weeks straight." He squinted at me. "Ah been ridin' the long line now fer nigh on eight years."

The rider stood up and mounted his horse. He threw a leg over the saddle horn and looked at the men seated on the ground and standing with shotguns back in the fields. "Now ah wanta tell ever' cotton-pickin' one o' you rams somepin'. This new skinner heah is a home town boy. He got more brains then all you mammyjammers put together. He's my frien' an' ah want 'em left strictly alone. We'll call 'em Dardanelle—make it up."

The men scrambled to their feet and again formed into squads. Behind me, Scarface groaned and rolled in the dust of the turnrow.

"Dardanelle, you stay heah with me. Blue Moon, you take this doby wagon back to camp an' sen' Cap'n Burr out. Tell 'em to brang his telephone. They's a sonofabitch heah tried to kill me."

I saw the jeep coming long before it pulled up by the water cart on the turnrow. I saw the captain get out, a short stubby man with heavy jowls and tobacco juice running down his chin. I saw the contraption, an old-fashioned telephone with a crank, and I saw the batteries and wires. As Stud instructed, I held the reins of his horse while he and three other convicts pinned the ex-trusty down, spread-eagle fashion, and sat on his arms and legs. I saw Captain Burr, now exhibiting a strange excitement, tie a wire to Scarface's foot and another around his genitals. I heard Scarface beg, at first, but after the captain had turned the crank, I heard him scream.

"Give 'em a long one," the rider ordered, and the captain turned the crank rapidly for some time. The screams from the tortured man were those from some other land. They were long, and low, and begging and pleading. And tobacco juice ran from the stubby captain's mouth and dropped on the naked body of Scarface.

Suddenly I turned away. I felt sick and weak and a bit

dizzy. I sensed a strange nausea creeping up in my stomach, a feeling that I had never before experienced, and I bent and heaved and finally vomited there on the turnrow. Faintly I heard the captain ask, "Who is *thet* sonofabitch?" and I knew he was speaking of me.

"Thet's my frien'," another voice said. "He's from Dardanelle."

The captain spat in the dust. "Maybe we got this thang on the wrong person," he began, but the rider stopped him cold.

"You don't fool with 'em, Cap'n. He's a home town boy." And then I saw that the rider had pointed his gun at the captain's midsection. "Peter Pincher," the rider called to a shotgun man standing nearby, "take my horse and go get Cap'n Jones."

The field captain squirmed. He moved his feet in the wet muck where Scarface had voided his bladder and bowels. "Now you lis'en heah," he said to the rider. "Ah'm cap'n o' this camp an' you jus' another ragged-assed convict. Ah gotta brother in the guv'ner's office in Little Rock, an' you gonna heah 'bout this."

"Thet's awright, Cap'n, but ah got this gun. Ah'm ridin' this long line an' you gonna stay right heah 'til Cap'n Jones comes." The rider turned to me. "Dardanelle, take them wires off'n Scarface's balls an' put thet 'phone back in the cap'n's jeep."

When the green Oldsmobile came to a stop behind the jeep, a short stocky man wearing a gray suit calmly stepped out and stood for a moment by the car door. His eyes shifted to all parts of the field and then came to rest on me, standing by the water cart. Uncomfortably, I felt him studying me. Finally he turned and walked to the limp figure of Scarface, there on the turnrow. He nudged the ex-trusty with the toe of his shoe, then, glancing at the long line rider, he asked absently, "You sen' fer me, Stud?"

"Ah shore did, Cap'n Jones. Cap'n Burr heah got a strange idee thet he's ridin' this long line. Ah want 'em out'n this fiel'."

Captain Burr started to speak, but the superintendent held up a hand. "Now jus' a minute, George. How many times do ah gotta explain to you thet Stud is ridin' this long line? When he needs ya, he'll sen' fer ya. An' he'll tell ya what he wants ya to do when ya get heah. Is thet clear?"

Captain Burr sputtered. "Now you looky heah, Cap'n Jones. They ain't no goddamn ragged-assed Arkansas convict gonna give me orders. Ah gotta brother in Little Rock an' you gonna heah 'bout this."

Captain Jones moved close to him. "Now, George, you know yerself thet you come into this place in a A-Model Ford. Yer drivin' a n'expensive car now. An' them ol' cardboard suitcases you brought in—you got good furniture now. Yer pay jus' don't cover all them thangs, George, an' you know it. Maybe you'd like to have a number down heah an' then you'd be more pleased to take orders from Stud? . . ."

Captain Burr hedged. "Now Cap'n Jones, ah didn't mean ah wouldn't corp'rate. If Stud heah wants to be in full charge, he can. Ah was jus' sayin'—"

"Maybe they's work back at the camp," Captain Jones suggested. He let his eyes wander to the jeep, parked on the turnrow.

"Shore, Cap'n," the stubby man said, and half stumbled, half ran to the jeep. He circled the vehicle back up the bar ditch and onto the road. In a few moments the captain and jeep had disappeared into a dust cloud, far across the fields.

"How's ever-thang else goin', Stud?" I heard Captain Jones ask.

"Aw, purty good, Cap'n. Ah had to tighten up one ol' thang. He didn't want to pay his union dues."

"What's the matter with Scarface theah? Ah thought he was makin' out purty good down heah."

"Went plumb crazy, Cap'n Jones. Tried to pull a gun on me so ah had Cap'n Burr rang 'em up. He'll still be able to pick a lot o' cotton though."

"What's this new skinner s'pose to be doin'?"

"Aw, he's a home town boy, Cap'n Jones. Ah'm thankin' ah might make a water boy out'n 'em."

"Well, whatever you thank, Stud. Turn 'em out trusty if you want to." The superintendent walked to the Oldsmobile and got in. As an afterthought he called to the rider and said, "Whyn't ya come over to the house this evenin' an' eat supper with me an' the wife?"

Hells bells, I thought. *Talk about convict power. Yeah, Stud, why don't you go over to the super's house. Just drop in any time. Maybe he'll let you make love to his wife, or use that telephone gadget on him, just for kicks!*

"Ah don't know, Cap'n. Ah kinda thought sometime today ah'd set some rabbit traps down by thet ol' slough at One Camp."

CHAPTER XII

ONCE the Green Hornet had pulled away, the long line rider mounted his horse and started toward the men in the field. When he was off the turnrow and some twenty paces into the cotton stalks, he turned in his saddle and called to me.

"Dardanelle, you'n work 'round the water cart an' take some out to the pickers. Gi' some to the shotgun an' rifle men too. Yer a do'pop now."

I watched Stud ride slowly and casually away. I watched him ride through the squads and, at one point, saw him fall from his horse onto the stooped shoulders of a picker beneath a heavy sack. I saw him pummel the picker with blows from the butt of the .45 he carried at his waist. I saw the picker, a lean man, fall and then rise and grab desperately at the cotton on the white rows. As the rider mounted his horse again, I heard him say, "You mammyjammer, you better get me some cotton. Y'all don't get me near 'nough."

I turned to the water cart and studied the awkward-looking contrivance. It was a one-axle affair with a water tank enclosed by a huge wooden box balanced between two iron wheels. At the front of the cart between two shafts an old mule stood dreamily, not even bothering to fight away the many flies that gathered in the mucous mess around its eyes and beneath its tail. I went to the back of the cart and saw that a wooden spigot came out from the tank and pushed its way through a hole in the box. Two buckets hung on the side of the cart, and I filled both. I picked up a dozen tin cups with wire hooks and placed six around the rim of each pail. Then, with a bucket in each hand, I started across the field toward the nearest squad.

"Hey, water boy, gi' me a shot o' thet water theah." I looked in the direction the voice came from and saw that a shotgun guard stood some twenty paces out from the squad I approached and that he was addressing me.

"I'll give you one in a few seconds. First I have to get this squad watered down."

"They al'ays get the shotgun an' rifle men firs'," he began to protest, but Stud heard his words from across the field and wheeled his horse and came running, threshing white cotton and stalk debris as he crossed each row. He fell from his horse onto the back of the shotgun guard, and the guard went down.

The long line rider kicked the guard from side to side, then placed a booted foot on the helpless man's neck. "Y'all didn't heah what ah tol' ya 'bout Dardanelle, did ya? Hey, Dardanelle, make goddamn shore thet this bastard is the las' peckerwood on Cummins Farm to get water." He climbed to the saddle and again rode away.

The shotgun guard scrambled to his feet and brushed the burrs and cotton leaves from his suntans. He picked up the shotgun and stood quietly. But once I had set the water buckets down in the center of the squad and no one came forward to take a drink, he told me obligingly, "You gotta say 'water' 'fore anyone's 'lowed to get out'n his sack."

"Water," I said, and some twenty-five ragged men threw off their cotton-sack burdens and rushed forward. They were bearded and dirty men, lean and hollow-eyed and even ghostlike. As they gulped the cool water insatiably their heads tilted back and their eyes lifted up, and their eyes alternated between blue sky and the inside of their cups. The water trickled out and around the corners of their mouths and into their beards, and there it mixed with the dust and grime on their faces, and some of the water dropped into the fronts of their blue denim shirts and onto the ground.

"Damn, thet's good," one man grunted. And from another, "You gonna brang any more 'round to this squad?"

"I'll be around again," I promised. "First, though, I have to go through the other squads. But I'll be back."

I hurried away to the water cart and hung the bail of a bucket across the spigot. I turned the handle and water spewed out—first steadily, then crazily. For a few moments the bucket filled, but suddenly the water came to a trickle and finally ceased altogether. I shook the handle of the spigot and rocked the cart back and forth. It was then that I noticed the wet ground under the spigot for the first time. Someone had deliberately emptied the water tank during my absence.

"What's the matter, Dardanelle?" I turned and saw Stud, sitting as usual with one leg thrown over the saddle horn. "Someone playin' jokes on ya?"

"Look at that," I sputtered, pointing at the ground. "What sonofabitch would do a dirty, stinking thing like that!"

The long line rider laughed. "Yer learnin', Dardanelle. Yer learnin'." He dismounted and came over to the water cart.

"What happened, Dardanelle, is this: Some shotgun man slipped up heah an' let this water out while you was gone. He turned it off when he seen you comin' to make it look like you done it. He wanted to jackpot ya fer what happened over theah with thet other shotgun man. But ah know these sonofabitches. Ah know how they thank, ah know how they drank, ah know how they stank. Ah know who's good people an' ah know who ain't. Now take thet ol' thang we give the toenail treatment today. He'd fink on his own mother. Jus' the other day up in Cap'n Jones' office ah saw a note thet bastard wrote tryin' to tell Cap'n Jones what all ah was doin' out heah in the fiel'—makin' these sorry sonso'-bitches pay union dues an' all. An' that sorry bastard we wired up, ah been after 'em a long time. He's a rape-o. Prob'ly tried to tell ya he's in fer burgl'ry. Hell, thet rat never burgled nothin' in his whole life 'ceptin' some little eight-year-old-girl's panties."

"Can we get more water?" I interrupted.

Dumfounded, the rider stopped in the middle of some-thing he had started to say. "More water! What fer? Hell, we'll be quittin' in three-four more hours."

"Look, Stud," I began, "like you say, there's no doubt a lot of pretty sorry human specimens out there in that field. But there's some solid ones too. And they're thirsty, Stud. Very thirsty. Now, do the ones who are pretty good convicts have to go without water because of the sorry bastards?"

The rider looked at me and smiled weakly. He turned his head and looked at the field and said, half to himself and half to me, "Ol' Thirty-One's out theah, an' Ol' Ardmore—Dardanelle, take this water wagon an' flog this ol' mule in the rear end an' go to Seven Camp an' fill 'er up. An' don't try to play rabbit nowheahs along the way, 'cause God can't he'p ya when ya do."

I climbed up on the wooden box of the water cart and turned the mule in the direction of Seven Camp. Stud waved his arm at a high-power-rifle man, and the man waved back. "Let 'em out," Stud called, and I flogged the mule out from the squads of men and onto the turnrow. At first the animal moved slowly, but then, thinking perhaps that its day was done, it hit a beeline at an awkward pace down the dusty roadway. From my perch on the wooden box I looked at the open fields and considered my surroundings.

Cummins farm, I thought. *This is a reality. I, a new man here at the Arkansas State Penitentiary, am actually sitting in the very center of the nation's roughest prison.* I shook my head to clear my mind.

Along my path I saw sunflowers, ripe and bent in the autumn heat, with swarms of bees working industriously upon huge petals. In the bar ditch, off to my left, I caught a glimpse of a covey of quail as they sneaked swiftly into the tall grass, the younger ones streaming along behind. *Man cannot create these things,* I said to myself. *He can only maim and kill and destroy and rip apart. He has a mind and can think and eat and fashion his own shelter. Yet he has not learned to live even as well as these creatures out here in this tall grass.* I thought of the day's events and the horrible scenes I had witnessed. *But man is still good—he has to be! Were he not, who then would have plowed up these fields and planted good crops for the creatures to forage in?* . . .

A dog barked and my attention was drawn to a grove of trees a half mile off in the distance. Below the trees appeared to be pens, and I imagined that these would be filled with bloodhounds. *No, I will not do that,* I decided. *I will not leave the mule and the water cart and the thirsty men and head for the bottom lands. I will have lots of time* . . . but I wasn't sure. Everything seemed too easy. At the side of the road a rabbit darted into the rich foliage of the underbrush. *Ironically*, I mused, *that rabbit doesn't hesitate for one second to head for the deep protection of the river bottoms.* I slapped a rein at the old mule and watched its hooves splash indelicately through the fine deep dust as we moved along.

When I returned to the long line, Stud met me at the guardline. "Dardanelle," he said, "whyn't ya jus' take thet cart on out to each squad an' let 'em he'p theirselves." It was more of an order than a suggestion.

"What about the cotton?" I asked. "Won't that knock a lot on the ground?"

"Goddamn the cotton," Stud yelled. "These sonso'bitches got more cotton down heah now then they'll ever get picked. Anyways, a percentage o' what's knocked out is jus' thet much more thet Burr an' his kind won't get in their bank accounts."

There was something about this man I admired. A rough, brutal sort of a man, no doubt, but one with an indefinable strength somewhere within. Nevertheless, I thoroughly recognized Stud for what he was as rider of Seven Camp long line. He wasn't merely *serving* time in the Arkansas State Penitentiary. Along with Captain Jones, who apparently catered to his every whim, Stud *was* the Arkansas State Penitentiary. In this domain, his every word meant law. And from all I had seen so far, that law transcended every other man-made law on the face of this earth—even those constitutional laws having to do with federal and state governments.

"Y'all comin' back aroun' this way?" a shotgun man asked as I pulled the cart into the squad he was guarding.

"You'll get a drink," I said, "but *after* the squads are taken care of, *not* before." I noticed that a thin old man in blues was regarding me seriously. His brows were dark and heavy, and his eyes were sunk so deep in their sockets that it was impossible for me to catch any particular meaning or expression.

"How much you brang?" he finally asked, wiping the water from his grimy beard with a forearm.

"Two fives, run together, forgery count," I answered.

"Where you from?"

"Russellville," he replied. "My ol' lady wrote me a letter an' tol' me 'bout you."

"Ma?" I asked, surprised. "Ma at the hotel?"

"Thet's right," said the old man, and abruptly he turned and went back to his cotton sack.

I tried to remember what Ma had said to me when I was in jail at Russellville. *They kilt my boy in this very buildin' an' they sent my man to Cummins fer life. Thet was 'way back in the late thirties an' he been down theah ever since.*

"You know Ol' Russellville?" Stud later asked me.

"No more than I've heard. His old lady brought cigarettes to me and my girl friend while we were in jail in Russellville. We spent some time in her hotel before we got caught."

"Ol Russellville's a damn good peckerwood, but he carries a lot o' heat. Tries to run ever' chance he gets. Thet's why he got thet shaved head an' red cap. Been playin' rabbit ever since he come down heah. Kinda funny, ah recollect one time back in the early forties Ol' Russellville slipped out'n his cotton sack. Crawled pas' the shotgun man guardin' the squad, crossed the guardline between the high-power men, an' hit the woods. They chased thet sonofabitch in the river bottoms all one night. He put black pepper behin' 'em to foul up the dogs, but them hounds jus' wheezed an' coughed an' kept right on chasin'. They shore had a workout. He swim thet river 'bout fourteen dozen times an' the bloodhounds did too. One time the ol' crazy thang slipped right up to the levee wheah the cap'n were standin' an' sneaked a cigarette butt the cap'n had throwed away. An' they couldn't catch 'em, thet was the funny part. So when the frost hit the groun' next mornin' they pissed on the fires an' called the dogs an' give up. But Ol' Russellville beat 'em back to camp. He come in, naked as a picked bird an' wet as a drowned rat, his goddamn teeth about to shake out'n his head. 'What y'all come back fer?' the cap'n asked 'em. 'Y'all shore mus' like our hospitality down heah.' All Ol' Russellville would say was, 'Got the willies, Cap'n—got the willies. Had to come back.' " The rider slapped his leg with the black hat. "Make it up," he ordered, and climbed on his horse. I noticed that the sun, now a red ball, sat on the treetops far over the fields to the west. "Take thet water cart back to the camp, Dardanelle," he said simply.

When I came back from the mule barn where I checked the rig to a convict there, the rank men were just filing into the mess hall. The yardman stood inside the door and counted the men as they passed by. The numbers started at one, and each man in blue called out a succeeding number as he went through the door. Occasionally, when a man lost the count or didn't count out in a loud enough voice, the yardman would slap him or push a fist into the man's face. I was one of those who didn't speak loudly enough, and before I knew what was happening the yardman had knocked me down. I saw his foot coming and I tried to roll, but it was too late. I caught the blow in my side and pain shot through my body. Then, as though nothing had happened, the line continued to flow through the door—seventy-eight, seventy-nine, eighty. I pulled myself to my feet and again joined the procession. I filed with it between wooden benches and the long table to the far end of the mess hall. And there, a few feet away, stood Captain Burr, laughing and joking with three trusties.

"Set down," the yardman ordered, and every convict in blue half fell upon the wooden benches. Sounds of metal and utensils filled the low-ceilinged building. Tops and bottoms was the general fare—turnips I had seen earlier, cooked unpeeled with the greens left on. Cornbread cold, and blackeyed peas swimming in weevil juice.

"Damn, this new skinner got some meat on his plate," a man facing me across the table said to no one in particular.

I looked at the peas in my tray and saw that a white worm, well-done and the size of my little finger, was lying on top of the pile. I also saw the weevils, hundreds of them, floating on top of the pea soup which surrounded the pile. Sickly I pushed the mess away and munched on the cornbread.

"Don't you want them peas?" someone asked, at the same time pulling my tray to himself. "Ah'm so goddamn hungry ah could eat the south end of a mule goin' north. You'll be too, once yer heah a while."

Stud came in from the side door we had counted through. When he entered, the mood in the mess hall became quiet and ominous. Captain Burr even ceased talking to the three trusties and watched Stud walk up to the yardman.

"Ah heah you hit one o' my men comin' through thet door."

The yardman looked befuddled. He glanced at the men in blue and back at the rider. "Which one, Stud?—ah didn't know—" but he got no further. He was on the floor and the rider was kicking him. Time after time Stud's heavy boots plowed at the ribs of the yardman. And each time the yardman groaned, until he could stand it no longer. The scream filled the building and was that of a man strangling in his own blood. Then there was silence and Stud walked to the end of the mess hall and spoke to Captain Burr.

"Ah thank y'all got a sonofabitch back theah on the floor thet's ready fer Bodiesburg. You'n put Screamin' John on his job." With that, the long line rider walked out of the building and into the night.

The captain shuffled his feet. He spat tobacco juice on the mess hall floor. Then like a madman he jumped up on one end of a wooden table and walked the full length, kicking off trays and sorghum jugs. The trays clattered and fell to the floor, turnips and peas and cornbread covering the men who were sitting on each side. And all the time the captain raged over and over again, "You mammyjammers don't get me nigh 'nough cotton today! You mammyjammers don't get me nigh 'nough cotton today!"

CHAPTER XIII

As we filed out of the mess hall and into the single barrack we counted again, and this time I made sure that I had the right number and called it out loud and clear. Screamin' John was the new yardman who counted us through, and he was still dressed in the blues he had worn from the field and was dirty and grimy and unshaved. A hundred and one, a hundred and two—singly we passed into a fairly large barrack crowded with cots pushed together in pairs to form double beds. Around the inside of the building were wooden bars, formed by hard oak two-by-fours nailed firmly together in horizontal fashion. Outside the two-by-fours, between the bars and the wall, a passageway ran completely around the inside of the building. Two gates, I noticed, were the only means of egress—the gate we had entered from the mess hall, and another gate which led to the front picket. I also noticed that every man went straight to a cot and sat down, so I found an empty bunk and quickly did likewise. And when every man took off his trousers and shirt, this I also did.

"Gettin' up," I heard someone say, and I looked around. Outside the bars a guard on the picket answered, "Get up," and I saw the man who had first spoken get up from his cot and go to the back of the barrack. Time after time this happened. "Gettin' up—get up, gettin' up—get up." I asked a convict sitting on the cot in front of me what that meant.

"You gotta come in this buildin' an' strip down to yer shorts, if you got any. If ya ain't yer jus' naked. You gotta get on yer bunk and stay theah 'til ya wanta go back to the toilet 'r play poker. But you gotta say 'Gettin' up' firs', leastwise thet picket man'll shoot ya."

"He'll shoot right in the building?" I asked, astonished.

"Heck, they don't care. They do it all the time 'round heah."

"Oh?"

The man raised an eyebrow and looked questioningly at me. "You ain't Cap'n Jones' man already, air ya? You ain't gonna say nothin' 'bout what ah jus' said?"

I looked at the man more closely and saw that his deep-set eyes were a watery blue. I also saw that the man was worried and even frightened and, for saying no more than he had just said to me, I thought it strange and a little ridiculous.

"Why should I say anything about what you've just said— whatever that was?"

He looked at me as though I'd lost my mind. "Why, to he'p get out trusty, o' course! To get ya a furlough!" After a moment he added, "But y'all ain't gonna say nothin' 'gainst me, air ya?"

"No," I assured him, "I have absolutely nothing what-soever to say against you, now or any other time."

He relaxed. "How much you brang? Yer from Yell County, ain't ya?"

"I drew five," I answered. "Yep, I'm from Yell County. Where you from?"

"Ah'm from Paris," he said proudly.

"Paris?" I asked, surprised. "Are there many in here from over there?"

"Shoot fire, ah don't know. They's men heah from ever'wheahs—Paris, Stuttgart, England, Greenland, Kingston, Lebanon—"

"Damn," I interrupted, "I must have fallen into a cesspool of international thieves!" I again looked at the convicts in their shorts seated upon the cots about the barrack.

He seemed annoyed. "Heck fire, thet don't mean they from overseas. They from towns in Arkansas—Paris, Arkansas; Stuttgart, Arkansas; England, Arkansas, an' so on."

"You been here long?"

"Shoot, no. Ah jus' been heah 'bout three months. But ah learned enough already to do my own time. Ah don't bother no-o-o one. Ah jus' on'y got the hide six times since ah been heah."

"Is that a pretty good average?"

"Fer some it is. Fer some it ain't. 'Pends on who ya air. Take you, fer instant, you got it made—lessen the rider gets kilt. You'n go up theah right now an' cuss 'em all out, even knock the yardman down, an' they won't do nothin'. But if somepin' ever happens to Stud, yer in trouble."

"What, really, is a do'pop?"

"It's jus' someone still in the buildin' like you air. He's kinda trusty, but he's still in rank. They trus' 'em to go 'round the gun men. Thet's 'bout all. He can't give no orders."

I thought over his words and the enemies I had unwittingly made during my first day at Cummins. Captain Burr, for one. He'd be after me the first time the long line rider stepped out for a moment. And the shotgun guard who had wanted to drink before any rank man. Even the tall ex-trusty might possibly remember that I held the rider's horse while they wired him up. But in this very building I was equally sure that I had made friends. True, I considered, there wasn't very much that any rank man could do for another. But one never knew. Trusties were entering and leaving the barrack almost every day. Ol' Screamin' John, the yardman, for instance. In a roundabout way I was the very man responsible for his getting that job. *To hell,* I thought, *my mind is tired and getting confused.* I decided to fight the entire mess just one day at a time.

Long before daylight we filed out of the barrack and into the mess hall. We stumbled between the benches and table and waited for the order to "Set down." The fare was cold oatmeal without cream or sugar, thin adulterated chicory coffee, and a two-inch slab of white bread. Jars of sorghum molasses dotted the tables from end to end. Down by the cast iron stove Captain Burr stood talking to another civilian, a huge man, as they turned back and forth, warming their hands and their buttocks.

"Who is that man?" I asked a convict sitting by me.

"Thet's Cap'n Colebiscuit. He's the 'sistant sup'intendent. They gettin' ready to whup someone."

As the convict beside me finished talking, I noticed that a strange quietness had settled over the mess hall. I saw the yardman and two other trusties come out of the barrack and down to the cast iron stove. The yardman handed Captain

Colebiscuit a huge leather strap, folded like ribbon candy. On one end of the evil-looking hide was a wooden handle, and this Captain Colebiscuit took hold of, expertly flipping the strap to its full length. I judged it to be about four inches wide and five feet long, and I sat chilled as I watched the captain slowly bring the long piece of leather back over his shoulder and test the ceiling for height. Then it came down on the floor and I heard the metal embedded in the end clang cruelly against the worn boards. I saw the yard-man call out a tall blond youth from the table, and I saw them walk slowly toward the stove and the waiting captains.

"Get down theah," the captain ordered. "Y'all get on his head an' feet." He indicated the two trusties who had first entered with the yardman.

Slowly the strap went back, all the way over behind the captain to touch the floor. Then, just as slowly, it started its journey back. Up it came, gaining momentum, and then it fell and jerked forward toward the captain's right hip. I heard the sound, as though an explosion had ripped the mess hall, and under the sound I heard the blond youth plead. "Oh, Cap'n, ah won't steal no more sorghum. Oh, Cap'n, ah won't—Oh-o-o-o, Cap'n—" And then the blond youth screamed. Time after time the long strap made its evil passage across the shoulder of the panting captain, and time after time the building shook and the mess hall exploded. I saw the blue pants go sailing away from the young man's buttocks, and I saw the faded yellow rags of his shorts pushed deeper into his flesh. I saw blood, and brutal carnage, and sweat on the mad captain's face. And then I hung my head and looked at my tray. I could watch no longer.

Oh, God, where are You now?
Turn east from U.S. 65 and journey down that gravel road.

We are prisoners in a barrack here beside the great levee. You cannot miss the spot. The camp is dark, but a fire is lit in a cast iron stove.

But don't come now. A blond young man has just died, his kidneys ruptured by the brutal strap of a savage madman.

And all because that hungry youth filled a two-ounce medicine bottle with stale sorghum molasses.

You do not visit hell?

So be it!

That evening in the barrack the yardman called me to the gate at the front picket. "You gotta package an' a letter from someone, Dardanelle." He pushed a small oblong box wrapped in brown paper between the two-by-fours, and a letter. I walked back to my cot and sat down. "They don't open your letters here?" I commented to the watery-eyed man across from me.

"Naw, they don't care who ya write to 'round heah. But you gotta leave yer letters open when ya send 'em out. They wanta make shore you don't say nothin' 'bout the place. Don't ever try to get any word out'n heah in a letter. They'll kill ya, jus' as shore as ah'm settin' heah."

I placed the package on the cot and looked at the letter and return address. The letter was backed to Violet at the state hospital at Little Rock, but the handwriting was strange to me. I started to rip the envelope open when the yardman again called from the front picket.

"Bible Back, the cap'n wants ya out heah on the front picket."

A man a few beds away from me laid down a Bible and slowly walked to the front. The lock on the gate clicked and the man passed through.

"Bible Back," I heard Captain Burr say, "y'all been readin'

thet goddamn Bible more'n y'all been pickin' cotton. Get down theah."

The scene that followed was a repetition of the one I had witnessed that morning in the mess hall, plus a number of others I had seen throughout the day. Time after time the heavy strap rose to the ceiling and fell. And time after time the captain giggled and spat on the helpless man. As the screams and the begging filled up the dilapidated old barrack, I clenched my teeth and determined that, no matter what, I would shut off my mind to the savagery there on the front picket. I tore open the envelope and read the few lines, scrawled on a single sheet.

Honey,
They're giving me shock treatments up here and I've got to have help. Honey, can you stop them? I simply can't take any more. Already they've given me seven, and they say I'm scheduled for twenty-one. Can't you do something to make them stop?

Violet

The body of the letter was written in her hand, and the last few words trailed off and were almost illegible. She had signed her own name, but I reasoned that a nurse or another patient had helped her find and address the envelope. I gritted my teeth and sat silently as I heard the thump of a body thrown carelessly back into the lockup. I sat for a long time, and my thoughts were hateful ones. Finally a truth dawned on me that I had not realized before. If I left Cummins—and certainly I could from the water cart job— and if I got away, I would still be separated from Violet as much as I was in the prison itself. In Little Rock the deputies would be waiting for me to make just such an appearance. *No, Violet, I can't make them stop, but I'll do what I can. Tonight, I'll write a letter to Ma and ask her to intercede.* I picked up the package and looked at the brown paper wrapping. Somewhere along the way it had been opened and thoroughly inspected.

"My dear friend," the note in the package said. "I met Violet the first day she came here to the state hospital. She is a dear sweet person, and she asked me to take this charm she was wearing and have it engraved for you. She instructed me also that, no matter what happened to her, you should have this neckpiece and chain." Signed, "A friend."

Slowly I lifted the lucky charm from its cotton padding. I picked a few pieces of lint from between the links of the chain and turned the bright object to reflect the light in the dimly lit barrack. With some effort I read the tiny lettering, and as I did so my thoughts traveled back to another time and a scene in the Russellville jail. . . .

Then you do believe in God!

Maybe I do. Maybe I don't. Call it god, call it spirit, or call it plain common horse sense. Whatever it is, I guess we all believe in something.

You mean like the moon out there and what you were saying about believing there's a man in it?

I guess. . . .

You seem so different now. You don't even talk the same.

That's because I am different, Violet. The man you saw in me outside this jail was a more frightened individual than I'll ever think about being, locked up, even under circumstances such as these.

Am I different?

Not much. You haven't been forced to change. You've only needed to adjust yourself to a new situation. Women are funny that way.

Are you afraid now?

No, not really. But I'm uncomfortable as all get out.

Then I'm not afraid. . . .

The watery-eyed man leaned forward and peered into the empty box. "Did y'all get a present from someone?" he asked.

"I sure did, old buddy." I turned the charm in my hand and absently studied it.

"Wail, what do the writin' say?"

"It simply says *With you I am not afraid*— and that is all."

He squinted at me. "Now thet's a brave thang to say, don't you thank?"

"Yes, my friend, it surely is. A very brave thing indeed."

CHAPTER XIV

ODDLY enough, time for me passed rapidly on Cummins Farm. Each day at Seven Camp was a repetition of the one before, but in human events every day was a different one with actions and horrors peculiar to that twenty-four-hour period. Although my job was comparatively an easy one, the long line stayed in the fields from sun to sun, six days a week and often on Sunday, and when I entered the barrack at night I was dog tired and slept as soundly as the bare wire springs on my cot would allow. I had little time to think of my sentence or to count the hours or minutes of any given day. Thus I continued, in a company of haunted men, of frightened men, of desperate and hungry men—hour after hour, day after day, week after week.

"Gettin'up—get up. Gettin'down—get down."

"Wipe thet grease off'n yer chin."

"Whata y'all down heah fer?"

"Fer stealin' cattle, Cap'n."

"To hell ya air. Y'all down heah to pick cotton."

"Get down theah."

In my first month at Seven Camp, eleven men were wired up, many were given the hide, and three were killed. I saw men maimed, their fingers broken over the edge of the iron wheel of the water cart. I saw men beaten and stomped and kicked. And then one evening, after Stud had given the make-it-up order for the day, I heard him call out the name of one man that the shotgun guards had deliberately run up and down cotton rows all day.

"Hey, Ol' Thang," he said to the frightened man, "you an' me gonna go back to Seven Camp a new way tonight. They's a bridge over heah thet needs fixin'."

As I rode the water cart back to Seven Camp that evening, I wondered what bridge Stud would call out one man to fix at such a late hour. A peculiar feeling came over me. The sky in the west was red, and then purple, and the men were quiet, and the only sounds were squeaking harness sounds and footsteps of men wearing rubber boots. As I checked the water cart rig into the mule barn, stars came out one by one in the eastern sky, high over the levee and woodlands. A light appeared in the east and the light was that of a full moon, orange and round, climbing above the trees of the bottom land.

During the evening meal, two men were whipped on the mess hall floor. As we counted through the barrack gate, three men were slapped and one knocked down. I sat on my bunk and was well aware of the strange quietness permeating the building. Then I heard my name. The yardman was calling me out to the front picket.

"Stud wants ya to go he'p 'em with a little job."

As the long line rider and I and two trusties passed by the mule barn, Stud pointed at a pile of shovels by a fence and ordered us to take one each. "We gotta hole to dig," he said simply, and led the way, down the levee and to the right, across open and unplanted fields. "Dig heah," he ordered, "four feet long an' plenty deep."

I then saw the man he had taken to "fix the bridge," his shirt ripped from his body, the print of a horse's hoof stamped deeply into his chest.

The man was still breathing—a grating, rasping, horrible sound. He was mumbling something, and blood and spit and a slimy mess issued from the corners of his mouth. With a feeling I had never before known, I dug where Stud had indicated. I threw the blade of the shovel into the soft loam, and the two trusties did likewise. As the hole became deep and awkward for more than one man to work in, we took turns, as Stud ordered. Then, as the two trusties picked up the dying man, I heard him say: "No-o-o-o . . ."

"Throw on some dirt, Dardanelle—goddamn, y'all look like yer gonna get sick ag'in."

When the spot where we buried the man was level and smooth and matched the surrounding terrain, Stud told the two trusties to take the shovels and return to Seven Camp. "You an' me gonna run my rabbit traps, Dardanelle." He handed the reins of his horse to one of the men. "Y'all jus' well take my horse on back an' put 'em up."

I followed Stud across the levee and down to a wagon road leading to the river bottoms. Neither of us spoke for a while, but finally Stud broke the silence.

"They's a lot o' rabbits in these woodlands, an' they gettin' good this time o' year."

"Who was he, Stud? Who was the man you murdered and buried alive back there in that four-foot grave?"

Stud stopped in the middle of the road and turned facing

me. One hand rested on his hip, a few inches from the butt of his .45. Behind him, to the east, moonlight came through the branches of a giant oak, and the effect of that moonlight was to form long streaks and rays across the grass and ruts of the wagon road.

"You'd bes' ferget thet," he said finally. "You don't know who he is, what he is, wheah he is. You don't know nothin'. You heah? Ah acted on orders an' done what ah had to." Then in a lighter voice, he added, "Hell, Dardanelle, you s'pose to be my frien'. Tell me now, air ya my frien' 'r ain't ya?"

"I'm your friend, Stud, but I'm not the friend of the man you've come to be."

"What's thet mean?" he asked, puzzled.

An owl hooted somewhere in the woodland.

"It means this, Stud. Most of my adult life I have hot-checked and swindled people. I have drunk and raised hell and had good times and, granted, some bad ones too. But all that I've done was more in the nature of high adventure than in hurting any particular individual. You're a lot like me, Stud, and this part of you I like. But somewhere along the way you have lost yourself. You've taken on the false character of another person."

Stud's hand moved closer to the butt of the .45. For a moment he stood frozen, almost statuelike. "Ah could put you in a hole right 'longside thet other peckerwood."

"I know you could, Stud, but I also know that you won't. You won't because you know that when you do you will have murdered the only true friend you ever had."

His hand moved away from the gun. "Tell me this one thang, Dardanelle. Ah got to know."

"Yes?"

"Was ah saw?"

"Not by me or the trusties."

"By who was ah saw?"

"I'm not quite sure, Stud. I don't really know. Perhaps that question should be addressed to Someone Else."

He lifted his hat and scratched his head. Then he took off his hat and slapped his leg and laughed loudly. "Hell, Dardanelle," he said at last, "you turnin' more Holy Roller then them Baptist people over in Gould! We gonna go back up by thet grave we jus' filled in an' you gonna say a few las' words over the body."

The snow fell from gray skies and the pea vines became wet and soggy. The leaves fell from the cotton stalks, but cotton remained. The blackbirds, flocks and swarms of them, rose and flew from the corn stubble and chattered away toward another landing site. Crows, from the edge of the timber, ventured into the fields and the edge of the campground, stealing whatever morsel they chanced to find. The men in blue, driven hard by the rise and fall of the leather strap, filled wagon after wagon with white cotton.

"Y'all don't hafta medicate thet cotton now," the captains screamed. "We gotta get it out'n the fiel'—heah, take this wagon over to the state gin an' run this'n over to mine."

"Hey, Ol' Thang, wipe thet po'kchop grease off'n yer chin an' get busy. Ah don't wanta see nothin' 'ceptn' buttholes an' elbows 'fore Santa Claus gets heah."

The cotton, now stringing loosely from brown burrs, was loaded with ice and snow. The ground, now spotted with icecaps, became damp and wet and finally muddy, with ice puddles filling the middles between each row.

"Run thet ol' thang out heah. He looks like he needs to be tightened up."

The men, dressed in ill-fitting clothes and wearing rubber boots without socks, strained and heaved through the mud and the slush and then formed into squads with heavy wet sacks lying stiffly across their shoulders. They dumped the cotton on high wagons and returned for more.

"Goddamn," I heard one say, "it's colder than a well digger's ass in a Klondike." He rubbed his hands together and looked longingly at the fire the captain and rider stood by.

"Run thet ol' thang out heah," I heard Burr say.

The man came out and stood with bowed head before the captain. His clothes were wet and mud covered his rubber boots.

"Ah got somepin' heah in my jeep thet's gonna he'p ya keep real warm, Iowa," I heard the captain say. From the jeep he brought forth a paper bag and ordered the convict to, "Take off ever' stitch o' them ol' wet clothes yer wearin'. Take off the boots, too. Y'all don't need them in thet ol' mud." He handed the man a pair of silk panties. "Heah, these gonna keep ya nice an' warm—now get out theah an' get me some cotton, you mammyjammer." The captain giggled and looked shyly at Stud.

The man turned to go, but Stud ordered him back to the fire. "Iowa, take off them goddamn panties an' put back on yer clothes." He looked at the captain. "Ah'm ridin' this long line, Cap'n Burr, 'r did you ferget?"

The captain spat in the fire and went to the jeep. He put on a heavy fleece-lined coat and sat bundled in the seat.

"Gi' me thet coat, Cap'n," I heard Stud say.

The captain chewed rapidly for several moments. Warm tobacco juice slid down his chin and matted in the grimy mess of a three-day beard. Slowly, then, the captain got out of the jeep and took off the coat.

"Give it to Ol' Iowa theah. Ah thank it gonna fit him lots better'n it do you."

The headline in a leading Little Rock newspaper screamed: HIDE ABOLISHED IN ARKANSAS STATE PRISON, and the men in blues quit working and stood around. Small fires dotted the fields each day, and conversations were joyful and filled with hope. A hundred thousand dollars lay blanketed across the land, stuck in the boles on the cotton stalks, dripping and wet and secure, where no man could ever spend it.

"Hell, they can't do thet to us," the captains argued. "We ain't got no solitary cells ner nothin'. How we gonna handle these men?"

"Pick yer own goddamn cotton," the convicts yelled. Gleefully they stood around, overly polite to each other but insolent to any person who remotely smacked of prison authority. I asked Stud what he thought the news meant to the Arkansas prison.

"Hell, thet don't mean nothin'," he said casually. "Thet's jus' politics. Thet happens ever' once in a while down heah. People outside thank they're abolishin' the hide an' all the time they're jus' polishin' the goddamn thang."

"Even if it's true, they'd have to build cells for solitary punishment, wouldn't they?"

"Chris', ah don't know. A man can't pick no cotton while he's in a cell. An' thet's what they want, cotton—lots an' lots o' cotton. Too bad this come right durin' this part o' the cotton crop. They'll be a lot o' pressure."

And pressure there was. Three days later five captains came out to the turnrow and threw hide from daylight to dark. They whipped the trusties and rank men alike. They downed Stud and they downed me and, "Oh, God, Captain

—I'll pour water all over this prison farm if you'll just stop pounding in that same spot on my rear end!"

But the whippings were mild, as though some particular agreement had been reached. No man received more than ten licks, and the whippings were of such a humane nature that several men didn't even bother to say "Oh, Cap'n!"

Stud said he didn't give a goddamn. "The skin on my butt is tougher then thet on the water cart mule, an' all you captains air doin' is ticklin' me to death."

Captain Colebiscuit laughed. "Yer all right, Stud. We jus' gotta little job to do an' we're doin' it."

Captain Burr scowled. "Is Stud gonna keep on ridin' the long line?"

"Shore he is," Captain Colebiscuit yelled. "He ain't started this goddamn rebellion."

"Then whata ya chunkin' thet skin in my rear end fer?" Stud was addressing Captain Colebiscuit, and I detected a hint of humor in Stud's voice.

"Cap'n Jones said whup 'em all, from the long line rider on down."

"Bullshit," Stud muttered, and rode out to the field and among the squads.

"Dardanelle, ah been thankin'," Stud said to me a few days later. We were sitting by a fire on the turnrow, and he picked up a stick and pushed it deeper into the bed of coals. "Ah been thankin' thet ah don't give a good goddamn if these men do any work out heah 'r not." He raised his eyes and squinted at me.

"They'll have to do a little," I said. I accented the *little*, but Stud was not listening.

"Wheah do ya thank men go when they die?" he asked.

"How would I know? I'm not God."

"You thought on it some," he insisted.

"Well, if I had to guess, I suppose there's something going on someplace—a force of some kind operating in the universe. But for the life of me I've never been able to figure out what or where."

"Me neither," Stud said. "Ah jus' can't see Ol' Whiskers settin' up theah givin' orders to ever'one."

"He isn't."

"Thet's what the Jesus-lovers say."

"Have you ever thought of looking for the answer in nature—through the birds and the bees and the flowers and the trees, so to speak?"

"Have you?"

"Some."

"What did y'all fin' out?"

"Nothing. I merely felt better."

"Awright then, so much fer thet, but tell me this. Why in hell would any sonofabitch be crazy 'nough to come down to a torture house like this'n?"

"Now *that* I can answer," I said brightly. "I've given the subject one helluva beating and I think I know."

"Yeah?"

"Yes, I sure think I do."

"Wail, goddamn it, tell me, Dardanelle. Don't jus' set theah!"

"Sex."

"Why?"

"Before I answer that, let me ask you this. Why aren't there hardly any women at all in prison, compared to the number of men?"

"How the hell do ah know? Yer tellin' me."

"It's because sex is more readily available to broads. Men have to look and to chase and to seek. Somehow they get all mixed up inside and take out their feelings in a social way. There isn't a man you see out there in that field that a good piece of tail wouldn't straighten up some."

"It'd shore he'p me," Stud admitted. He slapped his leg with his hat. "Goddamn, Dardanelle, you all right!"

I grinned. "But what is all this talk about dying and where we go? I've got enough hell right here in this long line to last an eternity!"

The rider looked sharply at me. "Let's take this long line and go to Oklahoma."

"Jesus Christ, Stud, are you out of your cotton-pickin' mind? You know damn well they'll catch us and, if ever there was a chance to get out of this rathole, it'll be gone forever!"

"Maybe yer right," he said, "but ah don't wanta ride this long line no more."

"All right, then use your head. You've got a hard ass, and they're going to whip you, but—"

Stud interrupted. "Ah don't care 'bout no hide. It's thet damn telephone ah don't want strung up on me."

"All right—all right, but let me continue. You know there's something in the wind. Why do you think they hit each person only ten licks the other day? The thing to do is just tell them outright and refuse to have anything to do with this long line. I don't know politics in Arkansas very well, but I'd bet my life that this is the time to get by with it."

"They got other ways, too. They could try me on some charges. Hell, these bastards might even gi' me the 'lectric chair fer all ah know."

"I doubt that. They want these stories to stay buried even more than you do. They aren't really interested in you or me or any other peckerwood here in this long line. Not enough to create a public scandal anyhow. They want money from these crops, and when you can no longer bring these crops out of the fields to buy them that money, they're going to drop you like a hot potato."

"Thet's what ah'm afraid of." He laughed and gouged at the fire with another stick. "Did ah ever tell ya 'bout the time ah screwed Cap'n Burr's ol' lady?"

I smiled.

"Wail, she don't look nothin' like thet sonofabitch. She's a young hillbilly gal, but she's purty as all get out. An' one day ah went over to his house to see 'em 'bout somepin' 'r other, but he were gone an' jus' she were theah by herse'f. They gotta daughter—Pattycake. You'll see 'er sometime. She comes down to Seven Camp an' dances on the front picket. The daughter do. Damn, she's a sexy bitch, thet Pattycake. She gotta butt thet'd stop a n'eight-day clock. Ah jus' been layin' off to hump 'er one o' these days. Anyhows, ah tells Burr's ol' lady, 'Imogene, ah'm a-gonna jackpot thet fat little husban' o' yourn if y'all don't gi' me some o' thet cute rear end.' An' she says, 'Stud, ah couldn't care less what ya do to my fat little husban', but if y'all wanta piece o' tail whyn't ya jus' come right out an' ask fer it like a man?' You coulda knocked me over with a snowball. Damn, she's a sweet little bitch. Tol' me she ain't had nothin' to do with him fer nigh on two years." He stood up and kicked at the fire. "Y'all rams make it up," he ordered.

CHAPTER XV

WHEN Captain Burr drove to the field for me, I was unprepared. I thought first that Ma had come for a visit. "Cap'n Jones wants to see ya," was all the captain would say as we rode across the bumpy fields to Camp Number One.

"Set down, Dardanelle," Captain Jones said, indicating a chair in front of his desk. He swiveled around to look out a window, and I took that opportunity to notice the clutter between us. On his desk was a strap like the one at Seven Camp. It was neatly folded and lying on top of an Arkansas newspaper, and elsewhere there were pistols and blackjacks and paraphernalia of every description. The superintendent, unlike the little field wardens, was cleanly shaved and dressed in a dark blue suit. A picture of a cotton crop, depicting convicts wearing clean clothes and smiling broadly, hung on the wall above his head. I noticed the lettering on the picture said simply, "1935—To the health and wealth of the people of The Great State of Arkansas."

"Whata they call ya Dardanelle fer, noways?" He did not turn when he spoke, but continued to look out the window.

"That's a name Stud hung on me when I first came here. It's the town in Yell County I fell from."

"How ya gettin' along out theah?"

"Fine, I guess, Captain, so far as I can tell."

"Y'all gotta fi', didn't ya?" He turned back to face me but fiddled with some item of torture he picked up from the clutter before him.

"Yes, sir."

"Y'all ain't picked no cotton since ya been heah, have ya?"

"Yes, sir, I've picked a little. I've helped men on their rows and I've picked off the ends around the water cart and doby wagon."

"Dardanelle," he said slowly, "whata y'all thank 'bout my prison?"

"Do you want the truth, Captain, or just an answer?"

He raised his head and his eyes met mine. That was the first time I had ever looked deeply into the eyes of the man who ran the Arkansas Pen. They were eyes I could never fully describe. They were gray eyes, gray like the dust shavings from pieces of cold steel. They were unreadable eyes, kind eyes, cruel eyes—eyes that were deep and sad and mysterious. *Those are the devil's eyes*, I finally decided. *They are like none I have ever before seen upon the face of this earth.* "Thet's all ah *ever* want, Dardanelle. The plain, unvarnished truth."

"Well, Captain, I'll tell you the truth. I think your prison is one of the greatest misfortunes ever perpetrated upon an otherwise fairly decent people."

He relaxed and again fiddled with an object upon his desk. "Y'all ain't afraid o' me, air ya?"

I casually rubbed my hand against the pocket of my

trousers and felt the lucky charm beneath my palm. "No, Captain Jones, I am not afraid of you."

"Y'all plannin' to do yer time?"

"Yes, sir. I'm planning to do what I can of it."

"Y'all wanta ride thet Seven Camp long line?"

"What about Stud? He's doing a pretty good job, isn't he?"

He turned back to the window. "Stud's awright, Dardanelle, but ah'm in kinduva rough spot right now. Ah got troubles from Little Rock from two directions. One direction says go light on the hide an' on'y hit ten licks. The other direction asks what in the worl' ever happened to this year's cotton crop. Ah need thet crop out'n the fiel', but ah can't go too rough on the peckerwoods while ah'm gettin' it out."

"Can't Stud handle the situation?"

"Stud's awright when ah turn 'em loose. But when ah hafta put reins on 'em, he falls apart. Stud needs a rest, somepin' like the mule-barn job fer a month 'r two. He'll snap back, after he settles down a little bit."

"And if I rode your long line, what would I be expected to do, Captain Jones?"

He seemed surprised. "Why hell, get thet cotton crop out'n under thet pile o' snow!"

"Any way I see fit?"

"Any way y'all see fit, Dardanelle. 'Course, y'all gotta keep all the heat off'n me ya can."

"Then tell Captain Burr that when I need him I'll send for him. And that goes for the others, too."

The superintendent seemed pleased. "It's all in yer hands, Dardanelle, from this spot wheah we're settin' on out."

"Will that be all, Captain Jones?"

He swiveled his chair back to face me. "No, not quite all. Y'all need anythang—anythang atall?"

"As a matter of fact, I do, Captain Jones. I need to visit

my girl friend at the Arkansas State Hospital in Little Rock."

From a side drawer in the desk he took a ten-dollar bill and handed it to me. "You'n have a twenty-four-hour furlough startin' now. We'll make some 'rangements to get ya to Pine Bluff an' you'n catch a bus out'n theah." He tapped his fingers on the edge of the desk and stood up. "But y'all had better be settin' deep in the saddle on thet ol' horse comes Monday mornin'."

Violet—Violet, what have they done to you now?

I climbed the stairs and came to your room and saw you sitting there. At first I thought I had made a mistake—your hair was swept back and you wore a smock and you did not look the same.

"The box—the box," you kept saying, and I glanced to my left and saw the contraption parked by a bench in the hallway.

The box, indeed. The little black box. One hundred and thirty volts on twenty-one different occasions. Or did they lose count and start over!

"They raped me."

That was in Russellville.

"Can't we go north?"

I'm serving time.

"The box—the box, will you make them stop?"

No, Violet, this is a guilt that must ride with me on my conscience to the day that I die.

After the men had filed out of the mess hall on Monday morning and lined up in columns of two, I counted each one. I wrote the figure on a piece of paper and buttoned the paper securely inside a shirt pocket of the bright new suntans I now wore.

"How many shotguns do I have?" I asked Screamin' John.

"You got thirteen. You need more?"

"How many high-powers?"

"Four."

Without a word I walked to a guard shack at the edge of the campground. A trusty handed me a holstered .45 and the reins of a saddled horse. I buckled on the gun and swung into the saddle. "Let 'em out," I waved to a man on a far corner of the campground, and pointed down the road to the cotton patch and the icy fields. As I passed the mule barn, Stud came out and talked to me for a few moments.

"Ah heah ya went down to Little Rock, Dardanelle. How was yer girl frien'?"

"Crazy as hell, Stud. She was crazier than you'll ever think about being." I nudged the horse with the heel of my boot and quickly caught up with the long line.

The men stood before me in the cold morning chill. Five squads of shivering, half-starved human animals—tired and weary but primed to the gills with every facet of hate imaginable. I held the men on the turnrow until enough light crept in from the east to risk putting them out in the open fields. Finally, when the morning shadows had lightened enough, I signaled the high-power men to take their stations, one on each corner of a forty-acre square.

"Fall out," I ordered, and men in blue scrambled to the wagons to take sacks and again form into squads for the short march down the rows.

Suddenly a lean boy called Johnnie Lee darted from a squad and onto the guardline. There he stopped and wrung his hands and turned in circles, crying. "Ah don't wanta go to the graveyard—ah don't wanta go to the graveyard."

I signaled the high-power men to hold their fire and rode

out where the boy was circling crazily. "Hell, I don't want to go to one either, Johnnie Lee. Come on over here off that guardline and build Ol' Dardanelle a nice warm fire."

The boy ceased crying and circled toward the water cart. He mumbled a word or two, but in a few moments a fire burst forth from the pile of wood he'd collected.

"Where are you from, Johnnie Lee?"

"Mesa, Arkansas."

"How much did you bring?"

"Twenty-one years."

"You were out trusty a while back—what happened to that?"

"Stud choosed me on it." Nonchalantly he bent down and straddled the bright flame.

"What in hell are you doing?" I asked, amazed.

"Ah'm warmin' my balls, good ol' long line rider. Ah'm warmin' my balls. Since ah been down heah this is the firs' time ah had this chance."

I smiled and rode away into the fields. I knew that Johnnie Lee would be all right now.

Captain Burr edged up to me on the turnrow and whimpered, "Did Cap'n Jones tell ya what bales ah'm s'pose to take over to my gin?"

"Captain Jones didn't say anything to me about you *or* your gin. He just told me to get this cotton out of the field and that's what I'm doing. Where it goes from here, I couldn't care less. You can stick the crop in your stubby rear end, so far as I'm concerned—*after* it's picked and on the wagons and away from here."

He looked wistfully at me. "You an' me gonna get along, ain't we, Dardanelle?"

"We sure are, Captain—so long as you handle your job and don't interfere with mine."

"Ah mean about the cotton, though?" He looked questioningly at me.

"Look, Captain Burr, if you steal all the cotton on this farm it's no concern of mine. Just don't interfere with my job while you're doing it. Now—while you're stealing, why don't you go somewhere across these fields and steal this long line a nice fat hog so we can all have a good dinner tonight."

He seemed pleased and hurried away. And that night we ate pork in the Seven Camp mess hall until Johnnie Lee became ill from the rich food and threw up all over the cast iron stove. The hide was nowhere to be found.

Screamin' John was a big man with pale blue eyes, a crooked nose and a loose-fitting set of broken dentures. He was anybody's dog who wanted to hunt with him, and his master was any man who happened to be in authority at a given time. But Screamin' John was one hellacious yardman. He'd have anything cooked on Cummins Farm—even the cotton sacks, if someone should bring them in and suggest that he do so.

"Dardanelle," he said to me that first evening in my new quarters above the barrack, "any time you'n get somepin' brought in heah to cook, ah'll have 'em cook it."

"You'd damn well better, Ol' Screamin' John."

"Was the pork awright ah had 'em cook today?"

"Fine, John, fine," I assured him. Then as an afterthought, "How in the world did you ever manage that?"

Screamin' John looked embarrassed. He scuffed his toe on the wooden floor. "Ah gotta little pull with Cap'n Burr. He brought it in on the jeep."

I went to my bed and piled in. I rolled over onto my back and thought of the day's events. At last my thoughts came to Screamin' John and the hog. I smiled and closed my eyes. My sleep was light but restful.

The next morning as I sat on my horse and waited for better light, I addressed the men. "Gentlemen," I said, "somewhere on this farm hens are laying eggs this very moment. Now the way I figure, if they lay real hard all day and don't stop for a noon-hour break, they might just possibly lay enough eggs to feed everybody at Seven Camp. Of course, I wouldn't want any of you to get the impression that I know where those hens are. Right this moment I don't. But I'm sure they're on this farm somewhere, because I've been hearing them cluck and cackle and crow. I'm equally sure that Captain Burr *knows* where they are. And if such a thing should happen that the hens don't want to keep on laying when he finds them, I'll simply tell him to bring us the goddamn hens." I signaled the high-power men to take their stations. "We'll do something like that, that is, if we get enough cotton out of this field today. Fall out."

"Johnnie Lee," I called to the lean boy. "How in hell is anybody going to be able to come up here and warm his hands if you don't build a fire?" The boy grinned and stumbled sheepishly toward the water cart. I took out a long knife I'd promoted for myself and whittled a new stopper for the water cart tank. And when the doby wagon came out at noon, surprisingly, the tops and bottoms had pork bones and pork skins and even a snout mixed in. I dipped a tray from the same pot and seated myself with the men.

I had taken only a few bites when I noticed that a man in blue was regarding me sullenly. I said nothing and continued to eat, but I secretly watched the man from one corner of my eye. Suddenly he jumped up and threw his tray in my direction. He shouted as loud as his lungs would permit, "Ah'm goin' home!" and headed for the woodland beyond the fields. High-powers exploded from the corner stations, but the man kept jumping the cotton rows and lunging straight on. I signaled the men to stop firing and mounted my horse. In a few moments I had circled the fleeing man and was between him and the woods. I pulled the .45 at my waist and sat waiting. The man stopped a few feet in front of my horse.

"Seminole," I said, "you must not like pig snout and good turnip greens and warm fires. I'm ashamed of you. Now you just stand right there 'til them ol' shotgun men get over here."

"Whyn't ya jus' go ahead an' shoot me an' get it over with. Thet's what they all do."

I ignored his statement. When the shotgun men came up I said to them, "Take this idiot back to the ranks and put him in Five Spot. Any bastard who can run through that hail of bullets and not get hit must be awfully shook up. I think he's nervous and needs a rest."

The shotgun men looked curiously at me.

"Have any of you men got different ideas?" I asked quietly, looking at each shotgun man in turn. When none spoke I added, "Then take Ol' Seminole back to that long line and make damn sure that not one hair on his head is touched." I turned my horse and rode back to the line and my flavored turnip greens.

"Ah heah y'all had one tried to get away," Captain Burr said later that day.

"That I did, Captain. That I did."

"What did ya do with 'em, Dardanelle?"

"That's part of the business of *my* job, Captain. By the way, we're getting lots of cotton out of these muddy fields. Why don't you pull that wagon there over to your gin?"

The captain grinned and squirmed pleasurably. He licked tobacco juice off his lower lip and spat on the ground. "Dardanelle, you all right—you all right." He started toward his jeep.

"Oh yes, Captain, I meant to tell you. Tomorrow there won't be any cotton for you to take to your gin."

He stopped in his tracks and turned slowly. "Whata y'all mean, Dardanelle? Whata y'all mean?"

"Well, Captain, it's kind of like this. We need two wash-tubs full of hen eggs. Now since we don't have them, I don't see how we're going to get very goddamned enthused about getting any cotton extra for your gin."

"Y'all need eggs, Dardanelle? Whyn't ya say so! Ah'n get eggs. Ah know—"

I interrupted him. "Now if it should happen that the hens aren't laying, just get the hens. Is that clear? And get them to Seven Camp in time for supper tonight."

"Ah know what y'all mean, Dardanelle. Supper'll be waitin'. An' see if y'all can't get jus' a little cotton out on tomarra's load." He shuffled away.

"How y'all doin', Dardanelle?" It was Stud, who had ridden out from the mule barn to see what was going on.

"Hello, Stud. Get down and fill yourself up on a cup of this hot coffee."

Johnnie Lee took his horse and tied the reins to a water cart wheel.

"Damn, thet's real coffee," Stud commented as he squatted

down and raked at the bed of coals around the pot. "How in hell did ya manage thet?"

"Just like everything else, Stud. Captain Burr's a fine man to work with. He's a better thief than I ever was."

Stud grinned and poured more coffee into his cup. "He should be good fer somepin'. He shore'n hell ain't no husban' 'r lawman." He took a swallow from the tin cup. "Heared ya had one tried to hit the brush."

"Yep, Ol' Seminole during noon break."

"Wheah is he now?"

"Out there in Five Spot."

"Fi' Spot! Goddamn, Dardanelle, thet's a telephone rap if they ever was one."

"Not now it isn't, Stud. Seminole's a tired man. He's off his rocker a little, but he'll pull out and make a damn good picker again—*after* he gets a bite of those scrambled eggs we're having tonight."

"You sonofabitch." Stud grinned. "You shore got Burr workin', ain't ya!"

We both laughed.

"Stud, I've been meaning to ask you for some time, what do you know about Captain Jones?"

He looked quickly at me, a side glance. He raked at the coals and considered my question. At last he said, "Ah don't know, Dardanelle. Whata ya wanta know?"

"Oh, where he's from, how he got to be superintendent, who he replaced, that kind of stuff."

"Wail, he's from thet area over 'round Paragould, an' he got to be super'ntendent when Cap'n Blueball died—'r got kilt, whichever way it actually were. Anyhows, Cap'n Jones come up through the ranks. He use to be a little fiel' warden kinda like Burr is now—on'y Cap'n Jones weren't nigh as goddamn sorry as Burr is." He again raked at the coals and poured more coffee. "Hell, Dardanelle, ah don't know what to tell ya 'bout Cap'n Jones. But ah'n shore tell ya a helluva lot 'bout Cap'n Blueball. He's dead now!"

I grinned. "All right, shoot."

"Wail, to begin with, Cap'n Blueball were the tobacco-chewin'est, hide-slangin'est sonofabitch thet ever walked on two stubby legs. In a way Burr reminds me o' him. He looks kinda like 'em an' smells kinda like 'em an' is jus' about as dirty an' filthy an' all. Anyways, under Cap'n Blueball we worked ever' Sunday in mud up to our asses. We eat worms an' weevils an' a few blackeyed peas an'—gawd, he were sorry. Then one day him an' some ol' trusty thang was out'n the jeep an' Cap'n Blueball fell over dead. So Cap'n Jones called up a Lincoln County jedge an' had twenty-one more years mailed to this ol' trusty thang, an' while he were at it he also called the newspapers an' had 'em come down to take pitchers. Never ferget it. They set the casket with Cap'n Blueball in it out'n front o' Seven Camp on the yard. An' they dressed ever' mammyjammer one o' us up an' made us march by thet casket. They made us look grieved while we done it, too. An' the nex' mornin' you shoulda read them papers. They had our pitchers in 'em an' the headlines said: 'Prisoners Mourn Passing of Beloved Warden.' Horseshit. Damn'd if we was. Ah never were so mammyjammin' happy to see someone have heart failure in my whole life!"

The dog man rode out past the long line.

"Stud got kicked by a mule at the barn an' he's dead as a doornail!"

"When did it happen?" I asked.

"Ah don't know. A little bit ago, ah guess. Ah jus' heared he got kicked an' thet's all."

The dog man rode on.

My God—My God, don't let them call me to cover him up. I didn't do it, Stud. On the gray hairs in my dear old mother's head, I tell you truthfully. I said not one word about any part of our conversations—today, yesterday, nor ever. I didn't think this would happen to you. I would have staked my life that it wouldn't.

Kicked by a mule! That's a good one!

Some day, Stud, we'll find you. We'll dig you up and the men there with you and we'll plant you all in a cooler place where the judges can sit in the shade of a blackjack tree and review your pasts.

My God—my God, don't let them call me to cover him up.

"The Gre-e-e-n Hornet!" I whirled in the saddle and looked at the shotgun guard who had yelled. He pointed across the fields toward the bright sunset, and after a moment I spotted the tiny silhouette of Captain Jones's automobile.

After the superintendent stepped from the Oldsmobile he stood for a moment and surveyed the squads working in the field. Satisfied, he turned to me and asked calmly, "How's ever'thang goin', Dardanelle?"

"Pretty good, I guess. How do things look to you?"

"Fine—fine," he nodded. He then added, "They got cotton wagons lined up down theah at the gin fer a half mile. Gotta go over 'fore too long an' jack them ol' thangs up."

"You want me to slow things down out here?"

"No—no, it's jus' about right. Jus' keep 'em goin' 'bout like they air—oh, by the way, Dardanelle, tell Ol' Burr to leave my chickens alone. He done got my ol' lady's fav'rite settin' hen an' she's raisin' Cain with me."

"I'll tell him, Captain, but we sure need more food at Seven Camp."

"Ah'll sen' over some 'taters."

"Fine, Captain."

"Need anything else?"

"I don't know. I've been thinking. Maybe we're missing the boat in some ways."

He glanced shrewdly at me. "How's thet, Dardanelle?"

"Well, you take a man like Ol' Russellville out there. He's pretty well done in. He's too old to pick much cotton and he's too damned contrary to run away. Why don't we send him home, Captain Jones? Men like him just hold the others back on their rows."

"Y'all talk to Ol' Russellville an' get 'em shaped up an' ah'll fix up the papers. The Parole Board can sign 'em later. Ah'll jus' give 'em a n'indefinite furlough." He went to the automobile and got in. As he pulled away he stopped for a moment and called to me. "Whyn't ya come over to the house this evenin' an' eat supper with me an' the wife?"

"I don't know, Captain. I kind of thought sometime today I'd set some rabbit traps down by that old slough at One Camp."

CHAPTER XVI

SCREAMIN' John touched my shoulder, and a rooster crowed. "Time to get up, Dardanelle. It's three thirty." He set a cup of coffee on the table beside my bed and moved to the door.

I threw off my blankets and came to a sitting position on the side of the bed. "There must be one chicken on this farm that Burr missed," I yawned.

The yardman laughed and started down the hallway.

"Hey, Ol' Screamin' John," I called after him. "Send Russellville up here on the double."

"Up heah?"

"Up here, Ol' Screamin' John, up here."

"Y'all wanta guard with 'em? He runs ever' chance he gets."

"You can walk him up, then leave us alone. I have some very important business to discuss with the man."

"Awright, Dardanelle, if y'all say so." He shrugged his shoulders and went away. In a few moments I heard the keys jingle and click in the lock on the front gate downstairs.

The man who came to my room was one I had said very little to during my stay in the Arkansas prison. He stood by the door at first and regarded me seriously, but after the yardman had left us alone he closed the door and said absently, "If y'all air thankin' 'bout turnin' me out trusty, ferget it."

"Why?" I asked, and indicated a chair for him to sit down.

"Fer lots o' reasons. Firs' off, ah don't hol' to no convict carryin' no gun over no other convict. Ah ain't thet kin'. Nex' off, say ah had a gun an' was made trusty, ah'd jus' hafta go home. Ah figure we're all animals, an' if ya put a n'animal in a cage it wants out. Thet's all ah ever want, is out." He twisted a knuckle into an eye socket and rubbed his heavy brow. "What ah'm sayin' don't have nothin' to do with you though, Dardanelle. Somehow 'r other, thet gun you wear fits yer hip. Y'all jus' seem to know how to wear it the way it's s'pose to be."

"You've tried to go home several times already, haven't you, Russellville? Didn't you drag into camp one morning after a night with the dogs on the river and tell the captains you had the willies?"

He grinned and I noticed his broken teeth for the first time. "Thet ah did, Dardanelle." He hacked and excused himself and pulled his chair closer. "Dardanelle, ah'n level with you." He glanced at the door and lowered his voice. "Ah had to come back. Ya jus' can't get away from them bottom lands. Ah knowed thet after ah were down theah a while, an'—shore, they couldn't catch me thet night, but they had me hemmed in. So ah figured the bes' thang fer me were to jus' play crazier then hell, an' thet's what ah done ever since." He glanced at me through bushy brows. "Ah'll tell ya somepin' though, Dardanelle. Ah ain't nigh as crazy as they figure ah am. Ah jus' been tryin' to keep livin'."

"Looks like you've succeeded."

"So fer ah have. Whata y'all got up yer sleeve?"

"Well, your wife Ma happens to be a very dear friend of mine. She tried to help my girl friend and me when we were in jail in Russellville. She brought cigarettes and bubble gum to us, and she gave us pills to relieve our pain. And since that time she has even tried to help Violet at the state hospital. Granted, there wasn't very much that your wife could do, but she tried."

"Ah know she did. Ah meant to tell ya 'bout 'er goin' to Little Rock."

"Oh, that's all right. I know pretty well what was going on. Anyhow, I don't want you to get the wrong idea. What I have done is for your wife more than for anyone else. You've got to understand that."

"An' what have ya done, Dardanelle?"

I handed him a paper I took from beneath my pillow. "I got you this release from the Arkansas prison."

He slowly reached with a gnarled hand and took the paper. He glanced at it, then back at me, then back at the paper again. "This is a n'indefinite furlough fer me." He seemed puzzled. "But who do ah gotta kill?"

"No one, Russellville. You're a free man now. They'll never call you back because there would be no object in doing so, and in a few days your permanent parole papers will be mailed to you at the hotel."

"But—but," he said shakily, "they jus' don't give these to people out'n they kill somebody."

"Look, you're an old man. You've been quite a bull in your day, but let's face it. What I'm telling you now is that you're no longer any use to the Arkansas State Penitentiary. You can't pick enough cotton. You're not wanted!"

"Then it's fer real?"

"It's for real, all right. But this you must also understand. No man in this world does anything for nothing, not even Ol' Dardanelle."

He looked suspiciously at me. "Yeah, what's thet mean?"

"It simply means this." I pulled an envelope from beneath my pillow and held it in front of him. "I want you to deliver this message to Ma."

"What is it, Dardanelle?"

"Well, right now it really isn't very much of anything. But she'll know what to do with it."

"A man likes to know what he's carryin'."

"All right then, I'll tell you a little about its contents. I have instructed Ma, in case something should happen to me, to mail this envelope to the Federal Bureau of Investigation in Washington. I have further explained to her that it'll do no good to send it to Little Rock, but with pressure from higher up the local offices will have to act. Now, in this envelope I have specifically instructed your wife to keep this message under lock and key, that my life depends upon no unfriendly eye ever seeing what I have written."

"Yer a cool cucumber, Dardanelle, an' ah like ya. As ah said, thet gun fits good on yer hip." He reached with a trembling hand to take the envelope, but I held firmly to one end of it.

"Will you deliver this envelope to Ma?"

"Y'all know ah'll do it, Dardanelle. Y'all knowed thet 'fore ya asked."

"Look me straight in the eye and tell me you will."

"Ah will."

I gave him the envelope and stood up. I watched him put the message inside his boot and turn to go. Then he turned back to me and the best I could tell there was mist in his tired old eyes. He stuck out his hand and shook mine. "Gettin' up," he said quietly.

As I came down the stairway and onto the front picket, the building exploded. The shot came from the runaround along the side of the barrack, and as the echo trailed off low groans and sounds of distress came from inside the lockup. Then keys jingled and trusties bustled about and the yardman called to the picket guard on duty.

"What'n hell's goin' on back theah?"

"Thet sonofabitch don't say 'gettin' up' 'fore he gets up."

"Wail, they s'pose to say 'gettin' up,'" the yardman declared. He yelled to the men in the lockup. "You rams better learn to say 'gettin' up' in theah 'r y'all be gettin' some o' what thet peckerwood got."

I stepped forward. "Goddamn all this palaver. Get those night men down here from upstairs. Get two extra guards on each side of this barrack, and bring that wounded man out."

Screamin' John looked stupidly at me for a moment, then came alive. He called the guards from their quarters upstairs, and he opened the gate to the lockup.

"Carry him out," I told two trusties, but when they did I saw that it was too late. A .45 slug had splattered into the man's chest and he was dead.

It was Ol' Iowa.

"Of all the senseless, harebrained, goddamned atrocities," I heard myself saying. I went to the picket runaround and started toward the guard who had fired the shot.

"He on'y done what he's ordered to," Screamin' John said.

I whirled on him. "Ordered to! I thought you had sense enough to tone these guards down. You know I don't go for this crap." I turned to the guard. "What do you expect to gain by something like this?"

"Ah gotta ninety-day furlough comin' now."

"Give me that gun," I said through clenched teeth, and held out my hand.

The guard, now unsure, placed the butt of the gun in my palm and started to speak.

"Screamin' John," I said, "I want this man stripped of these suntans and thrown in the lockup. His ninety-day furlough will be spent in One Spot, and I don't want to see his face behind another gun so long as I'm in charge here on Cummins Farm."

"But, Dardanelle—"

I cut him short. "Listen, Ol' Screamin' John, if you don't want your goddamned rear end thrown in the lockup too, you'd better get moving. And another thing—when they bury Ol' Iowa, where in hell ever that happens to be, I want a marker put up over his grave." I started to leave the building, but on second thought I turned and addressed the men in the lockup. "From now on you men are free to get up and down as you please. You can also visit back and forth with each other however you wish. Just make damn sure that you keep your hands off these wooden bars. One of these trigger-happy idiot sonofabitches out here on the picket might try to exchange your life for a ninety-day furlough."

Captain Burr stood on the turnrow and shivered. "They ain't much cotton left out theah, is they, Dardanelle?" He whimpered the words and spat in the fire and turned his buttocks in a better position to absorb the heat.

"Today's the last day, Captain. We start cleaning bar ditches Monday morning."

"Ah was hopin' ah could get a couple more bales this year," he whined. He rubbed his buttocks and looked at the men in the field. "What's thet ol' thang sangin' out theah 'bout?" He indicated a man in blue working a few feet away on a cotton row.

I lifted an ear to catch the words.

"*They's a town in Mississippi wheah a little filly dwells. . . .*"

"Sounds like something about Mississippi to me, Captain."

He looked questioningly at me and then frowned. "Mississippi? What's thet mean?"

"Nothing, Captain Burr. It's just a name in a song he's singing."

The captain inclined his head and listened for the words.

"*Ah thank ah'll go an' see her 'cause she's wearin' tinkle bells. . . .*"

"Y'all heah thet, Dardanelle? Thet ol' thang's sangin' 'bout runnin' off. Y'all thank ah oughta hit 'em ten 'fore he do?"

"Naw. He's just singing, Captain."

"But if he's thankin' 'bout goin' to Mississippi maybe ah oughta stop 'em 'fore he starts."

"He'll be all right, Captain."

"Wail, whyn't he sang somepin' 'bout Arkansas? *Pick thet cotton, eat them peas*—somepin' like thet, Dardanelle?"

"I don't know, Captain. I've got my mind on something else."

He looked at me quickly. "Yeah? What y'all thankin' 'bout, Dardanelle?" He twisted to warm his genitals for a change.

"Well, here it is just three days before Christmas and it looks pretty dreary down around Seven Camp. We haven't got a stinking thing for a Christmas dinner."

"Ah'n get y'all some sweet 'taters."

"Oh, I'm not worried about that. I'm thinking more about you, Captain, than anything else."

"What y'all thankin' 'bout me fer?"

"Well, I'm not really. I'm thinking about what they do

with all this cotton after they take it over to the state gin."

"Why, ah know what they do with it, Dardanelle. They make nylon an' rayon an' all o' them kinda fancy thangs out'n it. They's one peckerwood workin' over theah gives my wife satin dresses all the time."

"Do they make silk too?" I asked, surprised.

"No, ah don't thank they make thet. Ah thank a worm makes thet 'r somepin'."

"You damn fool," I said disgustedly. "They don't make a damn thing over there out of cotton but cotton."

He spat in the fire and twisted his rear end. "Wail, ah know they make cotton sacks 'cause ah seen 'em."

"They probably do make those, but think of the ginned bales they store in the warehouses waiting for better prices."

"Whata y'all tryin' to tell me, Dardanelle?"

I chunked up the fire and poured coffee in two tin cups. I handed one to him and sipped from the other. "All right, Captain, it's like this. I've got some friends working over there in those warehouses, and right this very moment a couple of them are holding a bale each of that nice ginned cotton. It's worth five hundred dollars a bale, Captain, and that's a lot of weight to expect those old convicts to keep on their shoulders very much longer."

He squirmed and looked pleased. "When can ah get it, Dardanelle?"

"As soon as you run two little errands for me, Captain."

"What air they, Dardanelle?"

"Number one—a nice beef, plump and round and not too old. You can take it out to the mule barn and Johnnie Lee and a couple of other old trusty convicts can skin it out. Number two—I want you to take five of the most staunch and dependable trusties that Cummins Farm has ever produced, load them into your jeep tonight, and go find a warehouse with a lot of good Christmas liquor. The men at Seven Camp are getting awfully thirsty."

"Y'all want me to do all thet, Dardanelle—fer jus' two little ol' bales?" He squinted at me and took a quick bite from a dirty tobacco plug. Then he swallowed more coffee.

"No, as a matter of fact I don't, Captain Burr. There's an old saying that the laborer is worth his hire, and you're indeed worth yours. So I've told another old friend of mine to hold up a bale for you—that is, in case you think you can get started right away."

"Y'all need beefsteak an' good liquor, Dardanelle? Whyn't ya say so! Ah know a whiskey store over in Desha County won't take a minute to get to." He hurried to his jeep and got in.

"Don't forget to bring Pattycake down to dance on the front picket," I called after him.

Christmas Eve night at Seven Camp was a ball. There was roasted beef and fried beef and stewed beef, and Ol' Seminole even had a bloody raw steak and ate it off the hardwood barrack floor. Pattycake came and we switched Radio Free Arkansas off the political news and onto a jitterbug jump. And the swingin' daddies from Dumas arrived with the booze—fourteen cases of guaranteed Scotch done up in pints and fifths and even a few sample bottles, plus eight cases of winter apples and a dozen sweet rolls.

"This stuff says guaranteed," somebody piped, "but we ain't a-gonna take it back even if it ain't no good."

"Y'all better believe it," a Dumas daddy chimed in. "We can't 'ford to!"

"Just a minute," I told everybody. "Those who want to

drink will have to go in the lockup to do so. There'll be no drinking out here. Now, open that gate," I told Screamin' John, "and have these cases stacked inside where the rank men can get them."

"Ah ain't gonna drank in theah," a trusty said firmly. "Them men'll kill me."

"Me neither," said another.

"All right," I told them, "you men can do guard duty for whoever else wants to go in and booze it up."

"Le'me have a bottle o' thet 'fore ya shove it in," I heard Burr say.

"You too, Captain—that goes for you too. If you want to drink, I'm sure that these men in the lockup will forget that you're captain and make you welcome tonight."

"Y'all ain't afraid o' 'em," I heard Pattycake say, and I turned and looked closely at her for the first time.

Yep, I thought, *Stud had her figured right. She's a sexy bitch. And like he said, she's got a butt that'd stop an eight-day clock.* I noticed that the wool skirt she wore came two inches above her dimpled knees and fitted her body snugly.

"Le'me in theah," the captain said, and stepped past the yardman and into the lockup. I grinned as he uncorked a bottle and took a long drink.

One of the trusties pulled out a harmonica and followed the beat from the radio. He held the instrument with curved hands and molded the music. He sucked at the low notes and made them whine. Then he released the notes from the palms of his hands and let them jump out into full rhythm chords. The music went wild.

"Ah know wheah ah'n pick up a guitar over in Gould. It's a-settin' on some people's back porch." A moment later I saw the trusty slip out and disappear, and I looked at Screamin' John.

"What they doin' back theah?" he asked worriedly, and nodded toward the far end of the lockup.

"Oh, they're just interviewing the captain," I said, "and having a good time."

Satisfied, Screamin' John continued to watch Pattycake. "Damn, lookit thet rear end, Dardanelle!" He clacked his broken dentures and his pale blue eyes became misty. "Damn, Dardanelle—damn!"

Pattycake's face became sweaty and red, but she was still cute. Her ponytail flopped as she twisted her hips and danced from one trusty to another, over and under their arms and down between their legs, and up to the next pair of waiting hands. "Ah gotta get some fresh air purty soon," she panted. "Ah'm jus' 'bout undone."

In the back of the lockup I heard Captain Burr giggle. "Come on, Ol' Screamin' John," I said, "we'd better walk down around the picket and check on things."

"Y'all boys know ah been good to ya," the captain said. "Ah got ya this beef an' good whiskey."

"We know ya have, Cap'n. We jus' wanta put these two little ol' wires on yer balls an' stick 'em in a light switch an' see how it feels."

The captain giggled and took another drink. "It tickles too much," he said happily. "Ooooh, thet *do* tickle too much!"

"Jus' once more, Cap'n. Jus' one more little ol' time."

I smiled and motioned Screamin' John toward the front picket.

"Take off yer blouse an' let's see what's makin' ya bounce like thet," I heard a trusty say.

"Aw, you boys jus' wanta see somepin' else," cooed Pattycake—but she blew them a kiss and took off her blouse.

"Gawd a-mighty!" said Screamin' John, and swallowed one part of his broken dentures.

A man in blue signaled me from the lockup. "Cap'n Burr wants Pattycake to come down to thet side over theah." He pointed at one side of the runaround near the spot where the captain was entertaining.

"Your honorable father wants you back there," I told Pattycake.

"Hey, yer cute," she said to me, and tickled me under the chin.

Screamin' John ended his coughing spasm and looked at me with red eyes. "She can't do nothin' back theah betwix' them ol' oaken two-by-four bars."

"We can't let her in the lockup," I said. "Those men would tear her apart."

"Hell, she doin' awright the way it is," a trusty said. "Ol' Cap'n Burr's collectin' a dollar a shot fer ever' swingin' john thet gets up theah!"

"Ah remember when ah used to take a gal to the haystack," Screamin' John said nostalgically. He wiped his eyes and continued. "Was up by Fordyce, it was. The moon come up an' we jus' kinda went walkin', she an' me. Ah couldn't say much an' she couldn't neither. We was too choked up. So we jus' walked, an' ah remember 'er palm got sweaty in mine an' then ah saw this haystack up ahead. An' we jus' both kinda knowed we was s'pose to lay down. An' thet's what we done. We jus' laid down on the hay in the moonlight an' she said, 'Don't,' but it were awfully weak how she said it. So we did. Gawd a-mighty, ah shore wisht ah had Pattycake up to my room right now!"

"Go to hell!" I said, and took a pint from the cases inside the lockup and went to my quarters. I poured a drink and tossed it down. My thoughts turned from Pattycake to Violet, who seemed very close. Then I poured another. *Violet, Violet, I need you—I want you.* God, how beautiful she was.

I held the glass up. *Violet, wherever you are, I drink to you. Goddamn a god-awful moment like this anyhow!*

I shattered the glass against the blank wall and fell on the bed. It was soft and the pillow molded to fit my head. After a long time I went to sleep.

CHAPTER XVII

THE long line rolled on. Dig those ditches. Clear that land. Don't you know that some day all these wooded areas along this river and around these fields will be rich farm land? No, Captain, there is no more cotton to give you. Now, in these final days of winter, there isn't even any snow left to sift the cotton from beneath. It is gone—the ice and the snow *and* the cotton. Particularly the cotton. It went away on the wagons. It blew away on the stinging winds. It is somewhere else now, in some warehouse or some factory or on the deck of some ship to a distant land. But there is still hope, Captain. The winter is lifting and this is a new year. The bar ditches are cleaned and one hundred acres of new land is cleared. Yes, we did that. We threw the mud and the slush and the rotten sunflower stalks from every ditch. We sloped the banks with our shovels, and we hacked and we chopped and we pried away any root that got in our way. Out in the woods we sawed down the elms and the oaks and the crazy bramble trees. We pulled out the blackberry vines and those of the possum grape and the climbing liana. We heaved and we coughed and we breathed white puffs onto a chilled air. But we took out the stumps from every acre. Look at the dark soil now, Captain! It is primed and seasoned for a new crop. Feel the March winds come in from the Gulf Stream? Those winds are good and determined winds. They are different from the fierce and unmerciful winds of the harsh winter months. And those are no longer snow clouds you see to the southwest. They are rain-heads. Lift up your face and taste the sweet breeze that travels in front of the rain-heads—forget last year's crop. It is gone. It is history. It is picked and ginned and wiped out completely. The bramble and the vines and the old cotton stalks are rolled up and burned.

Only the ashes remain.

Chris', Captain, there probably isn't even a record left of that crop. Not even a weigh sheet!

But there is still hope.

"Dardan-e-l-l-e, heah come someone from towards Camp One."

"Who does it look like? Is it the dog man?"

"Ain't no dog man. He don't ride like thet."

"Must be Captain Jones' runner."

When the rider drew closer I saw that he was the man who had signed me in when I first entered prison. Short and rotund, he sat low in the saddle and rode quietly.

"Cap'n Jones wants ya to come to his office tonight after ya take the long line in."

"What does he want?" I questioned him.

"Ah don't rightly know, Dardanelle. Cap'n Jones don't never say nothin' to me 'bout his bus'ness. But they's somepin' in the wind. They're openin' One Camp nex' Monday

an' they're bringin' a bunch in from Tucker. All hard shells."
He twisted his short body around in the saddle and looked
hopefully at me. "Maybe he's gonna put ya on One Camp
long line."

"I don't know," I mused. "I just don't think so."

"Why not, Dardanelle?" the little man asked encourag-
ingly. "Y'all done a good job out heah."

"That's just it. The job I've done out here is too good.
Somehow I feel that all my achievements are gone on the
winter wind."

"Ah do know they're brangin' a rider from Tucker," he
volunteered. "Maybe he'll be takin' this line an' you'n get the
hard shells at One Camp."

"Who are they bringing over?"

"Ah thank it's Bull Bates, but ah ain't shore."

"What kind of man is he?"

"Wail, Bull been down heah since he were 'bout seventeen.
Firs' he jus' had short sentences, but he kep' comin' back.
Las' time he robbed 'em a taxi driver an' got 'em a craw full
o' time. He saved Cap'n Jones' life once, ah know thet fer
certain."

"What does he look like?"

"Oh, he's 'bout forty-five an' bald on top. He's kinda
av'rage in buil' an' don't say much." He leaned closer and
spoke confidentially. "Ah can't say much neither, but Bull
Bates don't ride no long line like y'all do, Dardanelle."

"Who'll be the captain at One Camp?"

"Thet'll be Cap'n Rumblefinger."

"And what kind of man is he?"

"Wail, he's Indianish 'r French 'r somepin'. Anyhows, he
talks kinds funny, 's what ah'm tryin' to say. He's from
Louisiana—New Orleans, ah thank—an' he jus' sorta sang-
song whines."

"Is he a tall man?"

"No—no, he ain't tall atall. He jus' kinda short, but he ain't fat ner nothin'." He scratched his head. "Come to thank 'bout it, ah thank Cap'n Rumblefinger's Cajun. Ah know he don't read ner write."

A man working in a bar ditch called to the runner. "Hey, little ol' fingerprint man from Cap'n Jones' office, how's my record stackin' up?"

"Awright, ah guess," the little man answered. "Ah don't have much to do with thet."

Another man called from the far side of the turnrow. "Y'all ever dug any ditches since y'all been down heah?"

The runner flushed.

"Pay them no mind," I told him. "They're just trying to be funny—some kind of warped humor."

What had Stud said? "*Ol' Thirty-One's out theah, an' Ol' Ardmore.*"

"Wail," the little man said finally, "ah'll tell Cap'n Jones ah seen ya." As he turned to go he looked at me and quietly added, "Good luck now, wheahever they put ya. An' don't ferget to keep prayin'."

I met Bull Bates in the office of Captain Jones. The Bull was a man of medium stature, clean-cut khaki dress, and a western-style hat he never removed from his head. His eyes, like those of Captain Jones, were gray steel. His voice was calm, with almost a nasal whine, his words limited. I quickly ːensed that Bull Bates would be a dangerous convict under *any* circumstances. Absently I rubbed my leg and felt the charm in my right pocket.

"Bull is ridin' the One Camp long line," Captain Jones said. He looked at me and his eyes cut deeply. When I said nothing, he continued. "Ah'm puttin' Screamin' John on the line at Seven Camp, an' you'n work with Bull up heah. You'n be his 'sistant. Thet awright with you, Bull?"

"Thet's awright with me, Cap'n. Jus' so ah know wheah we stan'."

Captain Jones swiveled to face the window. "Awright then, ah'm brangin' all the hard shells from Tucker Farm. Ah'm also pickin' up all the red caps an' hard cases from the camps heah at Cummins. We gonna make this one hot jumpin' camp. Thet's what ah made it fer. An' this year we gonna make one o' the god-awfulest cotton crops thet's ever been made in Arkansas." He hesitated for a moment. "Guv'ner McWhitney done gi' me the go-ahead."

When Bull Bates and I left the office of the superintendent, he motioned me to one side. He ran a gloved finger alongside his nose and looked directly into my eyes. "Now ah don't know exactly who y'all air, but ah wanta tell ya this—don't monkey with my bus'ness. Y'all heah, Ol' Thang? Ah'm runnin' the long line. Ah'm runnin' the mess hall. Ah'm runnin' the cotton crop, an' the commissary an' ever' other thang 'round heah. An' if y'all cross me jus' one time, ah'll have ya pullin' a fourteen-foot sack thet y'all ain't never gonna get filled up." He walked away.

For several moments I stood there, not knowing which way to turn.

When the storm struck, it tore up Cummins Prison Farm. The lightning knocked down the vegetable shack and the winds ripped at the mule barn. The black clouds rolled and boiled, and the huge raindrops battered out peas from every tray. The horses ran in the wind and lathered along their flanks and foamed at the bits, and their eyes grew red and fearful. Then the winds died down and the lightning ceased, but the black clouds remained. And under those clouds, the hide rose and fell again, endlessly.

In May, the clouds went away and the sky paled and the sun glared down. The cotton plants, now pushing their seeds before them, worked through the baked crust and spread two leaves to the hot sun. The pea plants reached with delicate tendrils to catch at any weed. The knee-high corn rushed and trembled as the hoeing men passed through it. And along with the hide came the gun butts and the hoe handles and the heavy boots, but the hide was the best thing of all, for it left no scars. The men screamed and the hoes clicked on the hard earth, and the dust filtered away in the sunlight. Then one day the Bull called to me and I knew that, from then on, I was only a rank man.

"Y'all ain't doin' no good out heah. Y'all jus' well catch One Spot on the lead row."

"He'n come out'n the fiel' ever' mornin' an' read me the newspaper," said Captain Rumblefinger.

"He'n do thet. But ah want Ol' Dardanelle to pick lots o' cotton. He ain't never picked none since he been down heah."

"Awright, Bull, if thet's what y'all say, but ah still want 'em to read me thet newspaper."

Whata ya say 'bout thet, Dardanelle?

Yes sir, Captain. No sir, Captain. You're right, Bull. I'll do my best. I'll lead One Spot out a little faster.

"Why does Captain Rumblefinger always carry pebbles?" I asked Ardmore one day.

"Thet's how he counts, Dardanelle. If y'all will notice, when we come off'n the yard each mornin' he takes a rock fer each man an' puts it in a certain pocket. At night, when we line up to go in, he has to have a man fer ever' rock. If he lost them rocks, he wouldn't be able to count nothin'.'"

"It's sure odd, how he stays in the field all day."

"It shore is. Stud at Seven Camp wouldn't o' let 'em done thet."

"Aren't those the most ungainly hands you've ever seen? His fingers look longer than his forearms!"

"They shore do. They kinda remin' me o' a chimpanzee's ah seen one time in a zoo."

"His nose isn't so short."

"Jus' like a n'anteater's!"

"Let's jackpot the bastard," I suggested.

"How we do thet?" Ol' Ardmore asked.

"Well, keep an eye out while you're hoeing for an extra pebble. Get one just like those he already has and give it to me. In the morning when he calls me out to read that newspaper, I'll slip it into his pocket. And what do you think that'll do to his count?"

"Screw it all up," Ardmore assured me, then laughed. "Thet's purty good. Ah like thet. Heah, how 'bout this one?"

Come on, Dardanelle, come on. Goddamn the conversation up theah in the front o' One Spot. Move 'em ooout, Dardanelle, move 'em out!

"Why doesn't the Bull ever take off his hat?" I asked Ol' Thirty-One.

"The Bull's a queer. A bald-headed queer. He don't take off his hat 'cause he don't want no one to see thet he ain't got no hair. Thet's his punk out theah on thet high-power. Whata y'all thank they sleep out'n the cook shack fer?"

"Y'all three rams—one, two, an' three in One Spot— y'all come on out an' get tightened up. Y'all ain't doin' nothin' but talk, talk, talk."

"Ooh, Captain, I'll stop talking and go to work. Ooh, Captain—g-g-god-damn, Captain! Oooooh!" I screamed.

"Y'all better get on down thet row. Y'all ain't no big shot 'round heah!"

"Whata y'all cry like thet fer?" Ardmore asked me when we were back in the field.

"To get less licks, I guess. How many did he hit you?"

"Twenty-seven."

"He hit me twelve."

"But thet don't become you, Dardanelle. Y'all was a damn good peckerwood on the long line at Seven Camp."

"I was a good one down there. I'm a good one here. What's that yelling when the captain whips me got to do with it?"

"It jus' don't become you, thet's all. Heah, le'me show ya a trick. When thet cap'n starts to whup ya, grab yer arm with yer teeth—like this, jus' behin' yer han' an' off a little to one side. Pain is psychology, an' if y'all bite yer arm exactly the same amount as he's poundin', y'all won't feel nothin'!"

"We do it ever' time," Ol' Thirty-One chimed in.

"Y'all mammyjammers come on back out heah. Y'all ain't got tightened up nigh 'nough."

. . . *thirty-nine, forty, forty-one* . . . "Oooooh," I groaned.

"How many'd he hit ya, Dardanelle?"

"Fifty-seven, I think."

"An' y'all didn't feel it neither, did ya, ah bet?"

"I don't know. My rear end's so knocked out of shape I feel like I've had a spinal block."

"If y'all wanta cry an' yell then it's awright. Me an' Thirty-One know this cap'n though, an' if y'all jus' *got* to say somepin' when yer down theah, call 'em a major instead o' a cap'n. He likes thet."

"He shore do," said Thirty-One.

Move 'em out, Dardanelle. Goddamn, move 'em out!

Whata ya doin'? Jus' standin' theah noddin' an' sleepin' on thet row!

"Come on out heah. Y'all still got some slack thet needs takin' out."

"Oh, Captain. Ooh, Major. Ooh Colonel. Oooooh, g-g-goddamn, General! I've had enough!"

The captain started laughing and threw down his hide. "You awright, Dardanelle. By god, you awright! C'mon over heah an' read me this newspaper. Now ah don't care nothin' 'bout no ball games ner social stuff. Ah want politics, jus' pure ol' Arkansas politics all the way through."

I limped to the shade of the water cart and sat down on one cheek of my rear end. I unfolded the newspaper and began to read.

"Ah don't want it word fer word, Dardanelle. Jus' tell me what it say."

"Well, General—"

The captain broke into uncontrollable laughter. "Damn, Dardanelle," he spit and sputtered, "y'all beat all ah ever seen. Wait'll ah tell my wife 'bout this!"

"Yes sir, General," I said, and he started laughing all over again. He doubled up and began to cough there on the turnrow, and right at that moment I took my chance and slipped the extra pebble into his side pocket.

"Anyhow, Captain, here's what it says in this newspaper."

"You call me General, Dardanelle. Ah like thet."

"All right, General, here's what it says. There's an old white-headed judge over in eastern Arkansas who is going to run for governor. He says that he thinks he'll beat McWhitney by a landslide."

"Hol' it, Dardanelle. He say he gonna beat McWhitney? Thet ain't right. Ain't nobody gonna beat Guv'ner Eli McWhitney. He gotta p'litical machine thet they ain't no white-headed jedge ever gonna be able to get aroun'."

"Here's something, General. It says here that the prisoners on Cummins had pork chops last Sunday for supper."

"Cap'n Jones done thet. Makes it look good down heah."

"It says they're going to build a pontoon bridge on the Arkansas River between Russellville and Dardanelle."

"Ah don't care 'bout no news like thet, Dardanelle. Jus' the politics, thet's all ah want."

"Well, it says that the major portion of the voters here in Arkansas live in the towns and the cities, but that more people live out in the sticks."

"What's thet mean, Dardanelle?"

"I guess it means that most of the people living outside city limits aren't registered to vote."

"It also mean thet the same people who voted las' time will vote the same in this nex' 'lection. Yeah, thet's what it mean. An' them people's what's gonna keep McWhitney in office fer as long as he wants to be guv'ner."

"Y'all make it up," the rider said, and I scrambled painfully to my feet and took my place at the head of One Spot.

The Bull went down the line and counted the men. Behind him Captain Rumblefinger also counted, but in a different way. As the captain passed by the squads of haggard men, he took pebble after pebble from one pocket and transferred them over to another. Finally, at the end of the long line, he stopped for a moment and contemplated the extra pebble.

"How many do y'all count, Bull?"

"Ah got one hun'erd an' fifty-one, jus' what we brought out heah."

"Wail, thet ain't right," the captain said. He looked wonderingly at the extra stone. He then walked down the long line and slowly shifted the pebbles again. Carefully he took each one and changed it from right to left pocket. When he had reached the end of the line, he looked doubtfully at the one left over.

The Bull sat on his horse and watched. "Y'all still gotta n'extry, Cap'n?"

"Ah shore have, Bull. They's a peckerwood missin'. Water boy, go fetch Cap'n Jones an' the dog man. Tell 'em we done got someone excaped!"

The dog man beat Captain Jones to the field. The anemic-looking little convict trusty came across the fields from toward the grove of trees and the wire pens, and when he arrived he was panting and spent. But he had the dogs. In the pack there were bulldogs, fox terriers, great Danes, bloodhounds, and one chihuahua. And the round-headed chihuahua bounced along behind the pack and barked dangerously. The big dogs fussed over a terrier in heat, and chased the small ones away. But the small ones came back. When the terrier in heat wandered off to smell at the base of a giant redweed, the dogs all hopefully tagged along and smelled at the base of the same weed. Some dogs sat and grinned, and the medium-sized dogs frolicked and scuffled around her. When the terrier bitch again wandered off into the fields, the pack sniffed and followed behind. But all the dogs made sure that they did not wander away too far. They were a vicious pack from Cummins Farm, committed for life to a great manhunt.

"Y'all better take them dogs an' run a circle 'round this heah long line," the captain said.

"Won't do no good," the dog man answered. "These ol' fangs air chasin' thet terrier bitch, an' she's in heat."

"Wail, do somepin'. They's a man excaped!"

The dog man went to the edge of the field and pinched a leaf from a ragweed. He pressed the leaf between thumb and forefinger and smelled the green mess. He shook his head and circled the long line, testing objects for any scent. "Ah can't seem to pick up no trail ner nothin'," he said at last.

Captain Jones stepped from the green Oldsmobile and stood for a moment regarding the long line. "What's goin' on?" he finally asked.

The Bull ran a gloved finger alongside his nose and answered. "Nothin' ah know of, Cap'n Jones. Ah counted these rams an' got one hun'erd an' fifty-one, but Cap'n Rumblefinger says thet ain't right, thet they's one man missin'."

"Ah got one stone left an' nobody to match it to," Captain Rumblefinger said stubbornly. "An' 'fore this long line moves a n'inch ah gotta have a man to match ever' pebble to."

Captain Jones walked down the line and counted the men. "How many y'all say ya brought out this mornin', Bull?"

"One hun'erd an' fifty-one."

"An' how many do y'all say ya brought out, Bert?"

"Ah say we brought out jus' as many as ah got stones fer heah. An' ah ain't got enough peckerwoods fer all my stones."

Captain Jones glanced shrewdly at Captain Rumblefinger. "Why don't y'all go on in, Bert, an' let Bull handle the long line countin'. Come up to my office in 'bout a n'hour. Ah wanta talk to ya."

The green Oldsmobile rolled away. And the dog man stood up from the pile of mule dung he was sniffing. The dogs went away, the bulldogs and the great Danes and the bloodhounds and fox terriers. And behind the pack the little dog bounced and barked, fiercely, dangerously.

The sun beat down and the iron wheels of the water cart milled the loam and the gumbo into fine dust. The rubber boots of the men sloshed through that dust and out to the fields. The cotton stalks stood high and spread oily leaves that, even in the waning year, continued to reach for the sun. And the green boles on the stalks became rusty and began to open, at first on the outer edges of the stalks, nearer the sun's heat, then down where the red wine stems began to turn brown from the summer's heat.

The Chairman of the Board came down, and like a fat porker from the superintendent's hog farm the porcine little man ran panting along the ends of the rows. "Move 'em out!" he shouted. "Ah wanta see these sonso'bitches workin'!"

"We gotta cotton crop this year, the finest in Arkansas hist'ry."

"We gonna keep ya, Ol' Thang. Yer time ain't nigh up. Heah, the circuit jedge fer Lincoln County done mailed y'all two more years."

"Oh, Cap'n, Bull Bates done raped my wife."

"Whata ya mean, Ol' Thang? How'n the Bull do somepin' like thet? He don't like no women."

"He done it on big-leg day, when she come to visit Sunday. He took 'er out'n the cook shack an' threatened 'er life with a cleaver."

"Get down theah, Ol' Thang. Ah'll teach y'all better'n to make up stories like thet."

Dardan-e-l-l-e, move them ol' thangs out. Get thet cotton. Run thet white gold up yer arms to yer elbows. Make one trip from the stalk to the sack take ten poun's. Get thet One Spot down them rows. Two Spot's pressin' hard on yer rear end!

"What do thet say in the newspaper theah, Dardanelle?"

"It says, General, that Judge Jonathan Berry will use the Arkansas State Penitentiary as his main platform in his bid for governor."

"Ah'll tell 'em what ah know," said Ol' Seminole. "Ah seen plenty since ah been in this madhouse!"

"Y'all heah thet, Bull? Ol' Seminole gonna he'p Jedge Berry get 'lected! Whata y'all thank we oughta do with 'em?"

"Ah don't know, Cap'n. Whata y'all thank?"

"Wail, if he ain't got no eyes ner no tongue he ain't gonna be able to see ner tell nothin'."

So they gouged out his eyes and they cut off his tongue, and in a few hours, there on the turnrow beneath a boiling sun, the Muskogee Indian was dead.

"Take 'em down thet away," the Bull directed, "an' make damn shore ya plant 'em deep enough so he don't raise no stink in all this heat."

"Water b-o-o-y, go get the dogs an' Cap'n Jones. We got two mammyjammers thet air missin'."

The lightning flashed and the rain fell. At first the drops were very small and far apart. Then the drops became larger and knocked out craters in the muddy gumbo. Eventually, the rain came down in sheets and torrents and blew stormily across the face of every man. The rider looked up worriedly at the sky, then back at the men. "Make it up," he said calmly, and rode headlong over a man who failed to comply quickly enough.

Captain Jones came, but no dogs. "The pack was let out'n their pen," he said, "but it don't matter. They can't track nobody in this flood noways."

As we counted into the barrack, trusty convicts armed themselves and left the camp. For miles around, so I was told, farmers came out of their shacks and their shanties with pitchforks and clubs and whatever hardware they happened to own. The search went on, and Radio Free Arkansas blared the news from the front picket:

"Two desperate convicts eluded their guards at Cummins Prison Farm and are believed to be headed toward Pine Bluff.

Ol' Stuttgart, serving life for killing his mother-in-law, and Ol' Fort Smith, a five-year man, are believed to be heading for the home of the lifer's ex-wife."

And sure enough they must have been.

The guards brought them in late that night, and the captains hit them a hundred licks each there on the front picket. Then they shaved off their hair and gave them a red cap and tossed them into the lockup.

"Run the Bull out heah," I heard the superintendent order. "An' run out ever' shotgun an' high-power man thet was s'posed to be guardin' thet long line."

"You sonofabitch," Captain Rumblefinger screamed at the rider. "Cap'n Jones put ya out theah to work them men, not to let 'em slip off on home furloughs."

Captain Jones addressed the entire group of trusties. "Ah give y'all good turnip greens an' good peas, special from any the rank men get, an' ah give ya good clothes to wear. An' y'all let these two sorry ol' peckerwoods screw me aroun' like thet. Ain't ya got no conscience atall?"

"We'll take care o' 'em, Cap'n Jones."

"Ah know ya will, after ah get through takin' care o' y'all." He ordered them all to the floor again.

Lord, Cap'n, ooooh God! They's fire on the turnrow o' this buildin' tonight!

CHAPTER XVIII

WHEAH air y'all from?" the Bull asked me
one day.

"Oklahoma," I replied.

"Thet's awright. They ain't nobody no goddamn good from
Oklahoma nohows." He rode away, but returned a few moments later.

"Dardanelle, ah want you to pick out five men an' take
'em over by Cap'n Jones' house an' cut down thet oak tree.
Jus' cut it up an' get it ready to haul into One Camp fer
firewood. You'n have Ol' Peter Pincher to shotgun the crew "

I called Ardmore and Thirty-One and three other men. I
moved the small squad to the guardline, and Bull waved
us free of the high-powers. As we plodded across the fields
to the superintendent's house. Ardmore told us a story.

"Dardanelle, did y'all ever heah 'bout the time over to
Seven Camp we cut off the limb with thet ol' thang?"

"Thet was shore funny," piped Thirty-One.

"Wail, we was workin' down in the river bottoms clearin'

lan' an' this big oak had to have limbs cut off it 'fore it would fall. It were the biggest oak ya ever seen, Dardanelle. Kinda like this'n we're goin' to cut now. An' when ah say a big oak, ah mean the mammyjammer kin' thet is gran'daddy to all the res'."

"It were shore big awright," said Thirty-One.

"Anyways, this one limb wouldn't come off'n the tree. It were 'way up theah 'bout forty feet an' nobody couldn't seem to hack it loose. So this one ol' shotgun guard said he could get it, so we said he couldn't—jus' to vie 'em on. Wail, the argument went on fer a while an' fin'lly we tol' 'em to go ahead on an' try, so he took his shotgun an' clumb up in thet tree wheah the limb were, but when he got up theah he saw he ain't gotta n'ax. So he starts to come down.

"Wail, we don't want 'em to come down. We want 'em to trounce on thet limb wheah we done sawed it an' try to break it loose. 'We'll toss ya up the end o' this rope an' a han'saw,' we tol' 'em, 'an' you'n throw the rope over the limb up above an' tie it to thet one we're gettin' off. Jus' let the loose end hang down an' we'n hol' ya up from down heah.' So this ol' thang got out on thet limb, but it still wouldn't break off ner nothin'. So we tol' 'em to stay on the limb an' reach back an' saw with the han'saw, an' thet's what he done. An' purty soon the limb broke loose with thet ol' crazy thang right on it, an' we turned the rope loose. An' down he come, shotgun an' all. Damn, it were funny. Thet shotgun exploded an' thet ol' thang fell forty feet an' hit with a plunk."

"He shore did!" agreed Thirty-One.

"An' thet's when the rider come runnin'. 'What'n hell y'all doin' theah on thet groun' all crippled up?' he asked the shotgun man. An' this ol' thang was jus' moanin' an' a-groanin' with his leg busted an' his ribs caved in. So the rider tol' 'em, 'You stupid sonofabitch. Ain't y'all got no more sense then to get on a limb an' to cut the limb off with yerself?'

" 'Take me to a doctor—take me to a doctor,' were all the ol' thang could say, but the rider jus' lift 'em lay theah. Gawd, thet were shore funny."

"It shore were!" Thirty-One chimed in.

"Wail," Ardmore admitted, "we gotta have a little fun somewheahs along the way. Otherwise we'd go plumb nuts."

"We shore would," said Thirty-One.

Yes, I thought, *you've got to have a little amusement somewhere along the way. You've got to mix it in with the harsh reality and work them together and somehow make the whole warped mess change the pace of your mind.*

I looked at the fields and wondered: *Is this the signal from Little Rock? Is sending me out here with a squad of men the first hint of an easing up? Is it a prelude to a change of field reign?* I couldn't tell. Certainly there had been no letup in camp activities. The hide still rose and fell and the men worked desperately. Cornbread and blackeyed peas was the fare. Tops and bottoms and oatmeal and chicory coffee. *No—no, Dardanelle, wait a little while longer. Wait for the sap to rise and go down in this year to come. Your time has not yet arrived.*

Captain—oh Captain, what have you done? Since I have been in your prison I have first-hand knowledge of sixteen men you have killed. I have seen many wired up on your infamous telephone, the fingers of eight men broken, a multitude whipped and stomped and beaten, and one outright mutilated and left to die. I have seen men forced to run down your cotton and pea rows, men who dropped from the flaming heat of your unmerciful sun. Those men never got up again, Captain. They died where they fell, and your old quack of a horse doctor signed a certificate for each one, and that certificate read in part: *He died with his rubber boots on from heart failure.*

Heart failure indeed! One hundred and twelve degrees worth!

You fools, don't you know that a man with broken fingers cannot pick cotton?

You thought you were pulling one on me when you forced me out of the Seven Camp barrack to help dig an unmarked grave for a dying man. But I didn't kill him, Captain. You and your kind did that. You killed them all and you crippled the rest and that is *your* problem of conscience so long as the grass grows and the water runs.

Violet is gone now. She died from the many "treatments" they gave her. Only the other day in a letter from Ma I learned that an innocent girl lies buried somewhere near Little Rock in a potter's field. And in a sense, Violet too lies in an unmarked grave. But I have a part of her still. I have a charm with a brave inscription that I carry with me and in my pocket at all times.

With you I am not afraid.

No, Violet, with you I am not afraid. And because of you, I will never be.

The seasons passed on.

"C'mon, Dardanelle, move this One Spot out. We gotta have more cotton." The heavy stalks, in some places five feet or higher, were loaded with a bumper crop. During the first few days of picking, the rider carefully watched each sack. "We don't want nary a speck in any sack," he warned us. "This is gonna be sample cotton an' it's gotta be clean." A few weeks later the gods thundered up Little Rock way and the long line moved out even more. "Get thet cotton. We don't care how dirty it is. You'n put anythang in thet sack but the water cart mule!"

Dardan-e-l-l-e, Two Spot's a-pressin' hard on yer rear end! Lead thet One Spot out, an' we'll drive Two Spot to ya! Hell, the way yer goin' Five Spot's gonna run over ya!

Sack after sack I filled with the long staples. Row after row I picked, field after field. "Come heah, Ardmore, an' catch number one in Two Spot. Ah want Caveman on thet row you got. Ol' Dardanelle ain't gettin' nigh enough shovin'. Ah want Caveman to push Ol' Dardanelle all the way into thet Arkansas River over theah!" Up my arms ran piles of cotton. Then, with one giant sweeping motion, my body and arms twisted around and met the hungry mouth of the sack behind me, and returned for more. My muscles ached, my vision blurred from the heat and the sweat, the saltless spit in my mouth became red with blood. *Water boy, water boy. God-amighty, won't that water boy ever get here!* I quit smoking and learned to chew. Then I quit chewing tobacco and chewed cotton stems and turned my cap to the side of my head to protect my face from the blazing sun.

"Goddamn," Caveman on the row beside me said one day, "all ah'n see ever'time ah reach fer a wad o' this stinkin' stuff is one great big pussy. Ever' bole looks thet away. Do y'all thank ah'm goin' crazy, Dardanelle?"

We both laughed and kept picking.

Christmas came, but no Santa Claus. The winds howled and the sleet pelted our faces. The horses' hooves crunched in the snow, and the rider's horse nuzzled and nudged at the backs of the working men.

Dig them ditches deeper, Dardanelle. We don't want thet ol' water to get out'n banks an' get on this nice new cotton crop we're raisin' this comin' year. We gonna make this nex' crop the mos' mammyjammer thet's ever been growed on this pea farm!

My hands gripped the hickory handle of the shovel, and my hands became blue and numb. My shovel worked rebelliously at the frozen earth.

"Pour thet snow water out'n them ol' rubber boots if they're leakin'. Y'all don't hafta carry all thet extry weight aroun'."

Gawd, General, how I long to hit you up side the head with this shovel!

"Roll on! Roll on! Roll on!"

The snows thawed and the shovels now bit more easily at the gumbo and loam of the ditch banks. The ditches were cleaned, and the banks sloped at a forty-five-degree angle, and the mud and slush piled high on the turnrows and roadbeds. The hide came down interminably, and the men screamed and worked furiously. And when the first dawn of spring appeared, squads of starving human flesh were hooked to the plows to break the land.

"Harness 'em up!"

"Get a-hold o' thet rope an' pull thet plow right down a straight line to thet tree yonder."

"You sonofabitch, yer better'n any ol' mule ever thought 'bout bein'!"

"My boot's leakin', Cap'n."

"Ain't y'all never emptied thet boot? Ah tol' ya to pour thet water out'n it las' winter!"

"It's a funny thang," Caveman told me one day, "a little farmer can plant cotton in this kind o' muck an' pet it to death an' it won't do a thang. But let these sonso'bitches broadcast seeds out heah by the han'sful an' ever' goddamn one'll grow a bale o' cotton!"

"Where did you fall from?" I asked.

"Ah fell from Little Rock," Caveman said. "Ah gotta story 'bout me in a magazine in the barrack. Ah'll pass it over fer y'all to read once we go in tonight."

According to the magazine story, Caveman was in the Marines. He had come home to a country life in the edge of the Ozark Mountains, and he had liked the woods and had found himself a cave somewhere back in the dark valleys. By night he stayed in the cave and slept, but during the daylight hours he came down to the farmhouses and, while the farmers and their wives were out in the fields working, Caveman stole anything he could get his hands on.

Well, finally Caveman left some tracks—enough tracks for a couple of state troopers to follow to within a few yards of his hideout. So he promptly shot one of the troopers and wounded the other and, somehow or other, ended up in the county jail in Little Rock. His Marine uniform kept him out of the electric chair and got him a double life sentence on Cummins instead. Seems that somewhere along the way he had killed an old man and stuffed his body into a three-foot hole.

And there was a girl, too—a girl that, according to the story, was the wife of a sawmill worker. I read on, but decided that the girl he was said to have been playing tootsie with wasn't the girl depicted in the story at all. The girl in the illustration wore an evening gown and held in her hand a highball glass!

Oh well, it was something to read. I rolled over onto my stomach and went to sleep.

The barrack lights turned on in my dreams, and I no longer saw rows of crabgrass and tortured men in the aisles between the cots, but heard distinctly the yardman's voice.

"Rise an' shine, y'all mammyjammers. They's bacon an' eggs waitin' in the mess hall."

The bacon and eggs turned out to be oatmeal and chicory coffee. The rising and shining became the scorching sun that beat down from a cloudless summer sky.

"Did ah ever tell ya 'bout killin' the cats?" Ol' Ardmore asked me one day.

Thirty-One looked over our way. "Yeah, get 'em to tell ya 'bout thet, Dardanelle. It were shore funny."

"Wail, it were down to Seven Camp veg'table shack ten-'leven years ago, an' they had a n'ol' thang they called Peg. Now this ol' crazy dingaling didn't have no leg, an' he thought he owned thet veg'table shack, an' they weren't nobody could do much o' nothin' out'n Ol' Peg goin' tellin' it."

"Thet's right," said Thirty-One. "He shore did tell."

"Wail, anyhows, they was cats o' all kinds out'n thet shack. They was tabby cats an' Persian cats an' tom cats an' Russian blues. They was the gawd-awfulest bunch o' ol' starved an' scroungy-lookin' cats out'n thet shack ya ever did see. An' Ol' Peg jus' loved 'em. When he washed turnip greens the cats jus' got right in with what he were washin' an' Peg didn't care. He jus' washed them too. So ah said to Ol' Thirty-One one day, 'Thirty-One, the firs' time Ol' Peg ain't a-lookin' let's you an' me take some o' them cats an' skin 'em out fer rabbits. These ol' trusties pay fifty cents apiece fer rabbits, an' if we cut off the heads an' the tails an' the feet o' these cats them trusties can't tell the dif'rence.'"

Thirty-One nodded his head. "Yeah, thet's what he said awright. Ah remember jus' like it was yesterday."

"Wail, we took them cats an' dressed 'em out a few at a time, an' Peg didn't miss 'em much at firs'. But one day he started lookin' 'round an' kinda wonderin' 'bout his cats. He stood on thet ol' peg leg an' tried to bend over an' sniff under thangs. Gawd, he were silly. But we knowed he were on to somepin' 'bout them missin' cats. So fer a few days we jus' sol' one now an' then an' didn't say much. But one day when he went to the mess hall fer somepin' we wiped out the bunch. We took all the alley cats an' even a n'old calico blotched-up thang an' skinned 'em out an' sol' 'em to the long line trusties, fifty cents each. An' you shoulda heard Peg squall, but he couldn't figure out nothin' fer shore. So he jus' kinda settled down an' looked all aroun' an' wondered what happened to them cats. But it were shore quiet in thet veg'table shack. You coulda heared a pin drop. An' we could wash turnip greens out'n any cats fallin' into the tub!"

"How many cats were there to begin with?" I asked.

"Oh, they was 'bout twenty-seven, ah guess."

"Thet's what they was," said Thirty-One. "Twenty-seven."

"Wail," Ardmore continued, "one day a high-power man rode over by the veg'table shack an' wanted some more o' them good rabbits we had been catchin', an' Peg heared 'em say it. An' holy mackerel, y'all shoulda seen 'em chasin' Ol' Thirty-One an' me 'round thet shack on his wooden leg! He gotta butcher knife an', damn, were he mad! Called us ever'thang but a milk cow!"

"He shore did," Thirty-One agreed.

"Is that all he did?" I asked.

"Is thet all he done? Hell, Dardanelle, y'all shoulda seen thet man's eyes. They was jus' glassy an' shiny thankin' 'bout them cats!"

"Did Peg tell the captain?"

"He shore did. He went flyin' to Cap'n Burr the firs' time he seen the cap'n pull on the yard."

"What did the captain do?"

"Thet's what's the funny part. He wired Peg up fer it! An' then them trusties knowed somepin' were haywire 'cause o' them missin' cats an' they started sniffin' aroun'. But we give Ol' Stud half the money an' he tol' the trusties thet any time me an' Ol' Thirty-One had rabbits to sell they better buy 'em. Gawd, them were good ol' days."

I tried to imagine how the cats might have looked skinned out like rabbits. I shook my head to clear my thoughts. "You guys are sure corkers," I said finally.

"Us guys air corkers? What 'bout y'all, Dardanelle!"

"What about me, Ardmore?"

"Wail, yer jus' kinda peculiar, thet's all. Like thet Christmus party at Seven Camp two-three years ago. Boy, thet were a good one! Ah shore wisht we could have another'n like thet. Y'all should write a book, Dardanelle."

"If I ever do, I'll be sure to put you and Ol' Thirty-One in it."

"Thet's what y'all oughta do," said Thirty-One.

"Write a book, or put you two in it?"

"Put us in it."

"Even if I didn't give you and Ol' Ardmore a part, nobody'd believe it!"

"Wail, y'all should at least write somepin'," said Ardmore.

"Y'all shore should," Thirty-One agreed. "Y'all shore 'nough should, Dardanelle."

"What air y'all down heah fer?" the Bull asked me one day.

"For forgery and uttering."

"Well, go to work then," he said. "They ain't no damn check-passers no good noways."

CHAPTER XIX

I⌐T WAS in early April when Captain Jones again called
me to his office. He came quickly to the point.
"Dardanelle, ah'm pullin' in the Bull an' ah want
y'all to take his long line. Air ya willin'?"

I too came quickly to the point. "No, Captain Jones, I am
not."

He swiveled his chair from the window and his steel-gray
eyes fastened on mine. "Why not?" he asked coldly.

"Captain Jones, you once told me that you like the truth."
I placed my hand on the charm in my pocket and looked
him in the eye. "I know that this is an election year. I also
know that the all-powerful McWhitney administration is
near its end. Judge Berry, with the talkathon he is introduc-
ing from the south, will reach the hill people and win. He
has publicly denounced the policies and methods applied in
this prison system. He can't change those policies and methods in a two-year term, but he can limit your torture and

hold your hide-slinging to a bare minimum and perhaps eventually make some kind of a change."

The superintendent looked warningly at me. "Watch yer tongue, Dardanelle."

I sat for a moment waiting for him to continue. Finally I asked, "Do you want me to finish telling you why not?"

His eyes bored deeply into mine, and they were strange and unreadable. After a long moment, he whispered threateningly, "Go ahead, Dardanelle, tell me why not."

"Very well." I tried to control my voice. "From a personal point of view, I am your pawn. I am to be brought from your closet and used on your chessboard whenever you feel that it is necessary to play a game that I fit into. But as soon as it's no longer necessary, I am left at the mercy of a long line rider and a little camp warden—who have no mercy."

Captain Jones did not move a muscle. Neither did he cease staring into my eyes. "Go on," he said quietly.

"I have been whipped and stomped. I have had yellow jackets stuck to my rear end, been chased down cotton and pea rows and starved for drink. I have been cursed and insulted and had reflections cast upon every relative that I ever had, and some that I didn't have. Now, because of a change in the political situation here in Arkansas, you call me forth to do you a favor—yes, favor, Captain Jones. That's what it is, a *favor* to you. It is nothing to me, because I have lived through the roughest part of my sentence down here and can finish the rest."

He relaxed and changed moods. He swiveled his chair to the window and looked out upon the windy fields. "An' other than yer personal point o' view?"

"Well, looking at things more broadly, I know that you are in one rough spot. The Bull can never push this One Camp long line through the months of near-civility that will precede this election and follow it—never without scandal, that is. You cannot afford scandal, but that is exactly where I am leaving you. I want to see for my own satisfaction how your cunningness pulls you through these coming years."

"Dardanelle, y'all tol' me one time thet yer not afraid o' me. What makes ya so extry shore o' yerself now?"

I glanced at the fist in which I now clutched the lucky charm and saw that my knuckles were white. "Because, Captain Jones, I have placed letters in the hands of certain friends, and those letters are to be opened and read in Washington in the event of my death."

He slowly rose from his chair and edged around his desk and stood for a moment behind me. I heard him remove a paper from a metal file cabinet and return to his seat. He glanced at the paper and half turned to face me. "What makes ya so shore Berry will win?"

"Because, Captain Jones, he has already stated that the Arkansas State Penitentiary will be the center plank in his campaign platform."

"Other candidates have also used thet."

"No doubt," I agreed, "but they were dancing before an electorate that was already established. Judge Berry will use the talkathon and reach the hill people, and enough of those will tramp out of the sticks to make the difference."

"An' if Berry should lose?"

"I'll bet my life that he will not."

"Y'all may have just done thet," he said calmly.

The result of my visit with the superintendent began to be felt the very next day. On three different occasions the Bull called me to the turnrow, and each time Captain Rumble-finger hit me an even ten licks with the hide. "Y'all ain't gonna be able to do 'nough work 'round heah," the Bull told me, and that evening as I counted through the barrack gate of One Camp the yardman knocked me down. I reasoned that the Bull was right. Even in the mild political letup in camp activities, the forces at Cummins would find a way to dispose of me forever.

Move thet One Spot out, Dardanelle! Pull them plows!

A bullet kicked at the ground in front of me and splintered a redweed stalk.

Stay calm, Dardanelle, I told myself, over and over again. *They will not kill you,* but I wasn't sure. I knew that on Cummins Prison Farm anything could happen to anyone at any time.

That night in the barrack I clutched the charm in my hand and buried my face in the hard mattress of my cot. I prayed silently, so no one could hear.

The crop was planted, and in that short interval before hoeing time the Bull took the long line down by the front gate of the prison to clear the trees from an old slough.

"Ah want y'all rams to fall off'n thet water an' cut down them trees an' brush. Then ah want y'all to bear-hug ever'-thang an' dash out heah with it on dry lan'."

The slough was oblong and covered some ten acres. The water was shallow generally, in the deepest places no more than four feet. But in the mess of the undergrowth, beneath the willows and among the cattails and rushes, the stagnant water was working alive with huge moccasins—venomous snakes as large around as a man's arm.

"Damn, thet's a big rascal," said Ardmore, as a three-foot stubby went swimming by.

"They won't bother y'all if y'all don't bother them," someone else said.

"Dardanelle, c'mon out heah," the rider called to me. "Ah got somepin' fer ya."

I glanced at the bank where he quietly stood by the water cart. I saw that he was regarding a squirming object upon the ground. As I sloshed through the shallow water near the bank and approached the rider he hooked a stick beneath the form of the dark object and threw it for me to catch. Instantly I warded off the impact of the huge creature and grabbed its rough body with my right hand. And luckily for me, the point where I caught the deadly moccasin was directly behind its head. Disgustedly I threw the smelly thing to one side and turned to go back to my work in the filthy slough.

"Thet's quick thankin', Dardanelle," the rider called after me. "Thet's durn quick thankin' fer shore."

"What do you know about Caveman?" I asked Ardmore one day.

"Wail, ah know thet he's a bloodthirsty bastard. Ah also know thet he's a good solid peckerwood, but thet he's awful dumb."

"Do you think he really killed that old man and stuffed the body into a hole?"

"Ah know he done it. He says so hisself."

"Does he have any relatives come down to visit?"

"Ah don't know fer shore jus' who comes down. Ah thank his mother's in Texas, but ah do know somepin' else."

"Yes?"

"Wail, while he were in jail in Little Rock they was this preacher come visited 'em. The preacher had a progrom on Radio Free Arkansas, an' he used to talk a lot about Caveman an' thangs. An' even now Caveman gets hun'erds o'

Christmas cards from all over the state. But ah don't know if the preacher comes down to visit 'r not."

When pea picking began, the first day in the field I looked at the pushrow man beside me and studied him closely. Caveman was a young convict I judged to be about twenty-four. In height he was five-nine, of medium build and dark complexion. His hair was black, his eyes dark brown, and in his speech I noticed a slight impediment—a tongue-tie, I guessed....

"Don't you have people who come down to see you?" I asked him. When he assured me that he did have, I questioned him further concerning his visitors.

"Wail, my mother an' two brothers come down from Waco, Texas—they moved out theah when Mom an' Dad split up a few years back. An' then they's this preacher in Little Rock. He come to my trial an' talked to people 'bout me on his radio progrum. He comes down, an' ah get 'bout fifty to a hun'erd Christmas cards ever' year. Ah get cards from people ah don't even know!"

"You like this place?" I asked.

He glanced at me, a woodsy shrewdness revealing itself in his brown eyes. "No better'n y'all do, ah don't 'spect." He pushed down a huge bloodweed in the pea drill.

"Do you want to do something about it?" I pursued.

For some time he picked quietly. Finally he answered, "If y'all air plannin' to take off, ah don't."

"Caveman," I said, carefully selecting each word, "if I were planning to do something like that I wouldn't be talking about it as a rank man out here in this long line. I would have taken that rider's job and, from that position, I and the whole damn bunch could have gone home. I'm too short for that however. But I'm willing to risk my life to make this hellhole a halfway decent place to do time in. You're also too short for running away, even with your two life sentences. You can't escape and live anything like a normal life in the free world, and the way things are going in here you'll never be paroled. So what's left? We're risking our lives every day anyhow, so why not go whole hog or nothing?" I watched him closely.

He wiped the sweat from his deeply tanned face and spat on the hot ground. "Whata y'all got in min', Dardanelle?"

"I trust you, Caveman. I trust you enough to talk to you, and you're the only one in this entire long line I can do that with. Just make me this one promise: If you don't want any part in what I suggest, say nothing to anyone—not even to your mother or your brothers or to that preacher when they come down."

"Ah don't say nothin' to nobody."

A light breeze stirred the pea leaves and a grasshopper clicked and flew from a dusty weed. Across the dark green sea I saw that the Bull was mounted and sitting on a far corner of the field we were working in. I also noticed that the Bull was observing a squad that was picking in tall grass near one end of the rows. Satisfied, I turned again to Caveman.

"Very well," I said, and cleared my throat. "Now, the other day in the Louisiana State Prison thirty-two convicts cut their heel tendons in a blanket protest of prison and penal conditions. The newspapers got hold of the bloody mess and splashed it nationwide across front pages. We can bring that same thing about here at Cummins, if I can get the cooperation and help that I need." I waited for him to comment, but when he said nothing I continued. "Now, there aren't thirty-two men in this entire prison system who, under the circumstances, could be organized to do that same thing. There are too many finks and rats and whiners. This system breeds them that way and, as you know, anything said out here in this long line reaches Captain Jones as though it were telegraphed. There's only you, Caveman. And there's only Ol' Dardanelle. But together, working it in the right way, we can be just as effective as those convicts down in bayouland."

"Y'all mean out heah in the fiel'?" he asked coolly.

"Never," I said emphatically. "To do something like that out here in this field would be the biggest mistake of our lives."

"Can y'all get the news out'n heah?"

"Frankly, I can't—not by myself. But together we can, through your mother and through that preacher with the radio program, and through anyone else who happens to come to the prison to visit you—*after* our heelstring boogie takes place, of course. And I've got a letter, placed in the keeping of a dear old friend, and in that letter are specific instructions to the federal authorities in Washington should anything happen to me here at Cummins Farm."

"Y'all thought on this fer some time, ain't ya?"

"Yes," I admitted, "for some time. I've waited, too, for the opportune moment. And this is it. If we cut our heel tendons in that barrack in the early morning, they'll never kill us. If we do it here in this field, we'll never see another sunrise."

"Why did ya pick on me?"

"Because you have guts."

"Dardanelle," Caveman said, "y'all got yerself one cold-blooded sonofabitch to back ya up."

I felt relieved, but said only, "I never doubted that for one moment, Caveman. Never for one pea-pickin' moment did I think otherwise."

"What y'all two mammyjammers gettin' so palsy-walsy 'bout?" It was the Bull who, somehow or other, had slipped up without my noticing him. Slowly the rider slid from his saddle and walked over and stood by me. Calmly he took out his .45 and pointed the gun at my head. "Dardanelle," he said, "y'all air the sorriest ol' thang thet ever come down to this pea farm. Now c'mon, Dardanelle, tell yer pushrow buddy heah jus' how sorry y'all really air." He pulled back the hammer on the .45.

Sweat ran down my face and blinded my eyes. I clutched at my pocket and the lucky charm. *Oh no, God,* I prayed. *Let me have one more day. Don't let it end like this.*

"Tell 'em, Dardanelle," I heard the Bull say.

"Caveman, I am the sorriest sonofabitch that ever hit Cummins Farm. I am lower than a piss ant and not half as important."

"Tell 'em how sorry yer mammy is."

"She's sorry too, Caveman. She's sorrier and lower than I am. All my relatives are lower than henshit and three times as nasty."

"Tell 'em who ah am, Dardanelle. Tell 'em that ah am the greatest."

"The Bull is the greatest, Caveman. He is life and death and, right at this moment, all creation."

The Bull lowered the gun and jammed it roughly into my ribs. "Dardanelle," he said meaningfully, "if yer in this fiel' when the sun comes up tomarra mornin', ah'm gonna let this hammer down, right through yer heart." He holstered the gun and sauntered away.

"Whew!" I heard Caveman say. "Looks kinda like he wants ya to take off 'cross them fields toward home."

"That's what it is, Caveman," I said shakily. "He has

signed my death warrant and my execution is set for the early morning. Are you still riding pushrow for me?"

"Jus' like ah said."

"Then I'll see you on the concrete floor of the barrack toilet just before daylight is breaking. That's when the blood runs the coldest—right when the roosters are crowing, and the men scramble madly into their clothing."

Despite Bull's twelve-hour stay of execution, I still had apprehensions. I imagined he might call me out, to go back to camp another way, to "fix a bridge" and to lie finally in a grave too short for me and unmarked. When he gave the make-it-up order, I took my place as number one man in One Spot, and I stood there and waited while the seconds ticked by and the Bull counted. *Oh God,* I again prayed, *don't—don't—don't. Let my stay be for a full twelve hours —full and free for our plans. Let them come true, oh God, let them come true.* To myself I also said other things, words that were crazy but somehow filled up the seconds and marked the time until finally I heard the Bull's voice. "Move 'em out," he called to the high-power men, and the long line eased forward. I heaved a sigh of relief and almost became giddy. I talked rapidly to the man walking beside me. Without really thinking, I commented on the orange colors in the western sky, and the green grass upon the shoulders along the roadway.

"Wail, whata ya know!" a convict exclaimed as we seated ourselves in the mess hall. "Tops an' bottoms! Ah ain't seen none o' them since the doby wagon come out'n the fiel' at noontime!"

"Ah could tell the smell o' these goddamn thangs a mile away," another one commented. "Hell, if ah'd a-knowed ah was gonna be gone this long ah'd a-packed a lunch!"

Someone changed the subject. "Y'all see the newspaper men out'n the fiel' this mornin'?" We all looked at the man who had spoken.

"Who y'all tryin' to B.S.?" a tall man asked.

"No, really—they really was. Y'all ask Ol' Thirty-One an' Ol' Flytrap, they'll tell ya. They run all o' Fi' Spot over behin' the levee an' made us change clothes. Then they run us up wheah the newsmen was an' they took pitchers."

"Lotta good thet'll do," said someone else. "They been doin' thet fer years down heah an' all thet happens is thet the Little Rock papers print stories tellin' how we flat got it made." He looked at the man who had made the announcement. "Ah bet after the newspaper people left they took ever'body an' made 'em change back into the same ol' clothes an' whupped ever'one thet didn't look happy while the visitors was heah."

"Y'all mammyjammers better quieten down," the yardman said. He was standing between the two rows of tables, studying every face.

On my cot in the barrack I thought of the day's events. The newsmen wouldn't mean anything. That was simply another gimmick that Captain Jones used to delude the public. Even if I went to the field next day it was doubtful whether the Bull would kill me or not. What they wanted me to do was make a run. Then they could shoot me quite legitimately and no questions would ever be asked. But what will happen, I asked myself, when Caveman and I cut our heel tendons? We'll be unable to walk and therefore useless in the field, and to take us out there the doby wagon will have to haul us out. With me traveling that route alone they would quite likely find some way to dispatch my remains to

Bodiesburg, but with Caveman and his connections outside the prison they wouldn't dare. But Captain Jones, I reminded myself, would do anything within his power to keep any news from leaking out from Cummins Farm. He would stop letters and lie and apply his smoothest form of psychology and put out feelers among the men in the long line. He would pet those who could help his cause and denounce those who could not. He might even try to stop visiting altogether. At least he would see and talk to any who came before Caveman ever did. I must not underestimate Captain Jones, I said at last, and rolled over onto my side and slept fitfully.

CHAPTER XX

A S THE men scrambled into their clothes the next
morning, I looked across the building at Caveman
and saw him nod. At the same time we both
headed for the toilet at the front end and to the right of the
barrack. Once there, as prearranged, Caveman went down
on the floor on his hands and knees and I grabbed his bare
leg below the calf. I brought the razor blade across his
Achilles tendon and felt it glide smoothly into the tight
flesh. I saw him jump from the shock of the parting tendon,
and I reached for the other foot.

"No more," he said. "One's 'nough."

Quickly I gave him the blade and fell to my hands and
knees. "Cut them both," I ordered. "I don't want anyone
running me across those fields on one leg."

At first I didn't feel the razor blade bite into my flesh.
Then it stung and the tendon parted and a shock ran through
my body. Just as quickly the blade bit at the flesh of my
other leg. And then it was over, and we both sat, steeped in

a puddle of blood that ran out onto the concrete floor and around the base of the toilet bowl.

Someone came in, and hurried out. The building tender came in, but said nothing. At a barred window the yardman stretched his neck and looked at us there on the floor. We sat quietly for some time, and I held my legs below the calves to stanch the blood flow. I saw Caveman do likewise.

At last I heard Captain Rumblefinger's voice. "Go get their jackets an' read 'em to me." Moments later I heard him cursing as he flipped the pages of our records, and a trusty mumbled to him. After some five minutes he came to the toilet window and looked in. "Y'all are two fine sonso'-bitches," he yelled. "Ah treated y'all good an' give ya nice clothes to weah an' y'all do this goddamn thang to me!" He turned and addressed the yardman. "Call Cap'n Jones an' tell 'em what happened. Go ahead on an' le'me know what he says."

The yardman hurried away, but soon he was back and mumbled something in Captain Rumblefinger's ear. "Wail, go call Doc Vet to come take 'em over," and at that moment I knew we had won. Had we not, after the telephone call to Captain Jones, Rumblefinger would simply have opened the barrack gate and killed us there on the spot.

A fuss took place at the front picket desk. The telephone jingled and papers fluttered for some time. A key clicked in the lockup gate and the yardman called to Caveman and me. "Y'all two come on out heah."

"We can't walk," I called back, and immediately four trusties came into the small enclosure.

"Put yer arm aroun' my neck," I heard one say, and when I did so I felt him grip my wrist and hunch his shoulders.

"Heah, le'me he'p," another one offered, and I hung between the two men as they turned sideways to edge out the toilet door and the barrack gate.

Out a side door of the building, a car was waiting. At the steering wheel sat a slim turtlenecked man in a gray suit, and across from him in the front seat sat Captain Rumblefinger. I assumed that the slim man was Doctor Vet.

The trusties eased Caveman and me into the back seat and the Bull climbed in beside us. And the moment the automobile rolled away from the building Captain Rumblefinger twisted his short form around and asked anxiously, "Is they any more gonna do this, Dardanelle?"

"Plenty of them, Captain," I lied. "Plenty."

"What'd y'all do this fer, Dardanelle?" When I did not answer, he added threateningly, "Y'all want me to get back theah with ya? Y'all better answer me!"

I exploded. "You can do what you want, Captain Rumblefinger, but the reason we did this is to protest ratty, stinking, despicable varmints like you!"

"Whata y'all mean?"

"I mean, Captain, that even the lowest dog cannot invent and carry out the animalisms that you do!"

For several moments the captain looked at me and his eyes glared. Then he turned in his seat and sat quietly as the turtlenecked man guided the car up to an unpainted frame building.

Trusties carried us in, and a convict who had studied some medicine took charge. "Put one in theah on thet table," he ordered. "You'n put the other one on this cot."

"Look at them sorry sonso'bitches," I heard Captain Rumblefinger whisper to Bull. "They the firs' ones in Arkansas hist'ry to do thet."

I was the first to undergo surgery, and I heard the turtlenecked man and the convict argue as to exactly how severed tendons should be pulled together and tied again.

"Y'all can't do thet with this light stuff, Doctor Vet. Ah tied these together down in Mississippi, an' y'all gotta use heavy strang."

I felt someone grip my right foot.

"Won't make no dif'rence," said Doctor Vet. "They's a mil' conclusion right down in theah an' these ten'ons can't get 'nough blood to heal noways. Might hafta sen' to Austrayly fer kangaroo ten'on. Thet's the on'y stuff 'heres to human flesh."

Captain Rumblefinger objected. "Y'all can't put nothin' jumpy like kangaroo ten'on in these ol' peckerwoods. They wouldn't stay 'round Cummins Farm fi' minutes if y'all done thet."

"'S on'y thang 'heres," warned Doctor Vet.

"Ah can't he'p thet," said Captain Rumblefinger obstinately. "Cap'n Jones won't like it. Costs too much money."

The convict medic produced a hundred-yard roll of 4-ply cotton cord. "This strang'll hol' 'em together fer all time to come."

"Ah'n get some fishin' line down to the barrack," a trusty volunteered.

"This strang'll hol'," the medic repeated.

"What y'all pullin' it through with?" asked Doctor Vet. "Eye of a needle's too small."

"Ah'n punch a hole with a needle, then pull it through with them crochet hooks."

"Awright," Doctor Vet conceded, and went to the side of the room and sat down.

Beads of perspiration stood on my forehead and face as the medic probed high in the calf of my leg with the forceps. Pain racked my being as the blunt instrument clamped onto the end of the contracted tendon. As the curved needle bit into the fibrous tissue and the crochet hooks jerked cord through holes that were far too small, I buried my teeth in my arm to diminish the pain. *God, won't he ever finish!* I gripped the edge of the table—hard, hard, harder. And then I passed out.

The ceiling tipped sideways and blacked out. The bare mattress beneath me became soggy and hot. In the stifling heat of the room my eyes focused again, and then blurred. The burning fever that raged through my body swelled my tongue and cracked the skin on my lips and face. Dimly I saw figures come and go, and one time I heard the convict medic say loudly, "He's gotta have penicillin 'r he won't make it." I tried to sit up, but someone held me down. Vaguely I became aware that words were issuing from my mouth, and I tried desperately to hear the words I was saying. *Oh God,* I thought, *how merciful and humane is unconsciousness—but how dangerous!* I tried to think of the words more clearly, but the phrases would not right themselves. Then a thought came to me and seemed to make sense, and remained. *Lack of awareness on Cummins Prison Farm is one luxury that a man serving time can never afford.*

I felt someone stab my arm with a needle, and I opened my eyes. I turned my head on the rough pillow and saw the convict medic as he left the room. I saw Captain Rumblefinger and two trusties standing beyond the bars—bars that were formed by two-by-fours and nailed together in the same manner as at Seven Camp. *I'm not in a room at all,* I said to myself. *I'm in a barrack, exactly the same as the one at Seven Camp!* I turned my head to the other side and searched weakly for Caveman. On a bed next to mine I saw him smile and hold up two fingers in a feeble victory salute. From far away his words came to me—"Ah didn't thank y'all were gonna make it, Dardanelle"—and I tried to say something to him in return. A full realization of what we had done then swept over me, and my head spun. *He has only one tendon severed; that's why he's feeling better than I am.* I rubbed my forehead and felt the dry skin beneath my hand. I picked at the rougher places and pulled away huge sheets and rolled them between forefinger and thumb. "Water," I called, and a mousy-looking little convict appeared at the side of my bed. He cupped a hand to his ear and bent low. "Do you want a drink?" I heard him ask, and a moment later I felt the cool water upon my tongue. "You'll be all right now," he assured me, and patted my shoulder. I lay there and looked at the little fellow. *Something unusual—something unusual,* I told myself. *Oh yes, now I know. You have no accent. On this sixteen thousand acres of muck and mud there is another person who is not from boll weevil land. I have met another of my kind. You are an out-of-stater!*

"I'm Jimmy," the little convict told me a few days later. "I'm the orderly up here."

"Where are you from?" I asked.

"Milwaukee, Wisconsin." He glanced at me and smiled. "Say, you've had quite a time. If it hadn't been for Doctor Vet you would have died."

"What happened?"

"I don't know exactly, but I do know that the doctor had Captain Jones and a number of little wardens out on Jones's front lawn, and that the doctor was shaking his fingers at them and laying down the law. It wasn't very long after that when Doctor Vet brought penicillin up and we gave you your first shot. Your legs were infected. You would never have made it without penicillin."

"What else did Doctor Vet do?"

"Why—I don't know." He seemed surprised that I should ask. After a moment he added, "I do know that Doctor Vet is leaving Cummins Prison Farm."

"What's the matter, has the good doctor signed all the phony death certificates that he can stomach?"

"Doctor Vet is an ignorant man, I know. He's an old backwoods general practitioner who has never studied or learned the later methods. Too, he has nothing here at Cummins to work with."

"And the phony death certificates?"

Jimmy glanced at the front of the barrack. He hesitated for a moment before he answered. Then he selected each word carefully. "Sometimes a man, because of a small mistake or error in judgment at some stage of his early life, can become enslaved to other men and be forced by circumstances to do their bidding for years to come. We convicts here on this farm are like that. Because of a careless moment at a particular period in our lives, we became enslaved to the people of this barbarian state, to men whose fathers held huge cotton plantations and slaves throughout these lowlands to the Mississippi."

"Hasn't your backwoods practitioner taken the oath of Hippocrates?"

"I suppose, but the men of this region are earthy, practical men. High-sounding phrases like *codes of medical ethics* mean nothing to them when faced with the dangers of immediate personal entrapment. In such instances they rely on the only form of reasoning they understand—that of an earthy practicality."

"You've taken quite a liking to these thieves and murderers, haven't you?"

"Not really," the little convict said shyly, "but I think it helps if we try to understand what's deep inside a man."

"How will Doctor Vet be able to break free of his captors at this late hour?"

"I don't know that he can. I have learned, however, that the men of this region will deal. They will forgive any wrong if they can find some tangible, personal reason for doing so."

"Well, tell your Doctor Vet that I thank him for saving *my* life."

"I'll do that," he said. Then, "What would you men like to eat? I have strict orders to give you good food."

The pork chops and sourdough biscuits were delicious. As I sopped the grease from my plate and rinsed the food down with black coffee, Caveman asked, "Do y'all thank he knows what he's talkin' 'bout?"

"That's hard to say. Maybe he does and maybe he doesn't —but this is for certain: The sound of his words is dear sweet music to these old ears!"

"Do y'all trust 'em?"

"Not as much as Captain Jones does."

"Do ya trust 'em atall?"

"No. I don't trust anyone here on Cummins Farm."

"Y'all trusted me."

"Did I?"

Caveman lay silently for some few moments and looked at the ceiling. When he spoke he propped himself on one elbow and leaned toward me. "What would y'all done if ah'd tol'?"

"You couldn't have."

He worked himself into a better position, then asked, "How y'all figure?"

"Because, before you could have reached the rider or any captain, Ardmore would have killed you."

His brown eyes flashed. "Y'all tol' Ardmore what we was gonna do?"

"No. But Ardmore knew that something was up and he had orders from me to watch you—at every moment."

Caveman lay back on his bed and again looked at the ceiling. In a little while he asked quietly, "An' what would y'all done if Admore would'a tol'?"

"There was a man in the long line who would have killed him. He knew that, but he didn't know who the man was "

"Ah didn't thank y'all went fer killin'."

"I don't, but I believe in self-preservation. I don't believe that a man has a right to kill even a fly. But to protect himself he can. And he can use any means in doing so that he deems necessary."

"What 'bout 'lectrocutions an' thet kinda stuff?"

"Have you read the Ten Commandments?"

"No, but Mamma read 'em to me one time an' ah remember thet."

"Do you remember the one that says, *Thou shalt not kill?*"

"Yeah."

"Well, it doesn't say under given or varied conditions or circumstances, but *Thou shalt not kill period.*"

For a long time he lay quietly and turned that over in his mind. Finally he again propped himself on his elbow and said decisively, "Y'all shore wasn't thankin' 'bout no *Thou shalt not kill period* out theah in thet long line. How do y'all figure thet?"

I laughed. "There's just one way to figure it, Caveman. I was wrong—biblicalwise, moralwise, and otherwise. You'll have to forgive me. Do you think you can?"

He said nothing but continued to look at me for the longest time.

The convict medic unlocked the barrack gate and the

little fingerprint man from the front office came in. He came directly to my bed and bent over me. "Dardanelle," he whispered, "Cap'n Jones tol' me to tell you thet if y'all say nothin' 'bout this heel ten'on bus'ness, thet neither y'all ner Caveman will ever hit another turnrow. He said say that y'all was workin' on a mowin' machine an' the blade cut yer heel ten'ons."

"Tell Captain Jones to go to hell."

For a few seconds the rotund little man stood and twisted his hands nervously. But as he started to walk away he looked at me and said quietly, "Wail, good luck, an' keep prayin'."

"Do y'all thank we got it made?" Caveman asked me about a week later.

"I haven't the slightest idea."

"It seems awful quiet an' ever-thang."

"There's always silence before a storm. We'll know more about it when a bit of strychnine comes in on one of those fancy steaks!"

"Y'all really thank they'd kill us now?"

"Did your mamma ever own an ol' red rooster?"

A glassy appearance came into his eyes. "Yeah, as a matter o' fact she did."

"Then there is your answer. I think, Caveman, that here on Cummins Farm the gods are likely to do anything at any time."

"Ah guess ah keep hopin' fer somepin' good."

I looked at him sharply. "You're a simple bastard," I said. "Why did you kill that old man and the highway patrolman?"

"Ah don't know," he answered, and became silent again.

Time passed slowly there in the hospital barrack on

Cummins Farm, but for me they were restful days. The psychological pain of *not knowing* was ever present, but the food was good and the trusties left us strictly alone. My tendons knitted slowly and my ankles became stiff from lack of exercise or use. "Ankylosis," the convict medic called it. "Ah seen this happen down in Mississippi wheah them peckerwoods couldn't hardly even walk atall." I decided to wait a few days and begin an exercise of my own, but the medic warned me in no uncertain terms that, at such an early stage, the tendons would break with the least bit of pressure. I continued to wait, and to eat, and to think.

Will they kill us? Will they kill us? They didn't in the toilet at One Camp when they first saw what we had done. That doesn't necessarily mean anything. It probably means that right at that time they weren't sure. They didn't know who was involved in our plot or what possible means of communication we had with the outside world. Naturally Captain Jones would go easy at a moment like that. And didn't they sew us up when they brought us here to the hospital? As unprofessional and primitive as their surgery and treatment has been, yet it indicates something. They've made us reasonably comfortable here in this hot barrack, and the food is good. No one has made any definite threats against our lives. They've wanted to preserve us a while longer. But Captain Jones is a shrewd man. He can sit on that throne and wait forever, if need be. He knows that sooner or later we have to get out of this hospital—and then what? Let me see, how would Captain Jones think from that front office in this election year? First off, he knows that I too can think. He remembers that I told him I have a letter placed in the hands of an old friend. That letter and Washington—he could never be absolutely sure. And there are Caveman's relatives, should they ever come down. Then there's the slight possibility that Doctor Vet issued a warning of some kind. No. Doctor Vet wasn't likely to have done that. If that old horse doctor said anything at all it was probably, "Y'all lay off'n me, Cap'n Jones, an' ah'll lay off'n y'all." It is obvious that Captain Jones wants no part of this tragic mess to reach the outside world. He has already plainly indicated that. He has sent the fingerprint man to outright say so! Yet from his point of view, he would weigh heavily two things: "Which is the greatest danger to me an' my pea farm—an ex-rider who has firs'hand knowledge o' murder an' theft, 'r the 'accidental killin' under these circumstances o' two ol' peckerwoods who tried to take off? The livin' ex-rider is the mos' dangerous," he would decide. "But how can two peckerwoods run with their heel ten'ons cut? They could jus' disappear, like maybe they got away, but thet's dangerous, too. An' if ah kill 'em otherwise, how can ah ever be shore who they've tol'—'r if Caveman's family will want his body to bury in Texas? Damn thet Jonathan Berry anyhows! Ah can't be shore jus' what his politics'll be. But ah'n stop all their letters to the outside worl' an' cut thangs out." Yep, let's face it, Jonesy ol' boy, you're in one helluva fix. And so am I. It's mind against mind, and you have the added advantage of being free to walk around. Now, the important thing for Caveman and me is to never let the least hint or indication slip from either of us that we doubt ourselves or our position. We must act sure at all times. We must weigh each thought and measure each word before we utter it. But Caveman doesn't always have the presence of mind to do that. Hmmm. What Caveman says now really doesn't make a difference anyhow. Didn't Captain Rumblefinger address me when he twisted around on the front seat of that car as they brought us up here? And didn't the little fingerprint man come di-

rectly to my bed with Captain Jones's message? What Caveman says won't amount to a hill of Arkansas peas in Captain Jones's way of thinking. The superintendent will be certain within his own mind that Caveman came along only for the ride; that I ribbed Caveman into cutting his heel tendon because I needed the extra protection his outside contacts might afford me. No, let Caveman say what he wants. It doesn't matter. But I've got to encourage the stupid bastard, to keep him in a crusading mood. I need his mother and brothers desperately. God help us all—what a mess! People out there in that free world will never believe that such things take place!

The picket gate opened and the trusties threw a dark shape onto the wooden floor. "R-r-ub b-bub—bub bub bub bub bu-bub," the dark shape said. Its under jaw chattered and I saw that it was shaking from head to foot. The thing kept bouncing around and moving toward the beds on the far side of the barrack.

"Get them supplies," the medic said, and the mousy little convict brought in two buckets piled high with cracked ice. He placed the buckets and a short canvas tarpaulin near the bouncing shape.

"Lay 'em on thet tarp like we done the las' one, an' sprankle thet ice 'long each side o' his body. That's the way. Now tie strangs aroun' 'em to hol' the ice in—good, good, thet'll take some o' the heat out'n his bones. He'll be awright, if he's gonna be."

"What happened to that man?" I later asked Jimmy.

"He got too hot in the field and passed out. I don't agree with this method of packing them in ice, but that's how they do it up here."

"It's been my experience that they simply leave them to die in the fields."

"They've brought several up this year," the orderly said. "They do every election year, more or less."

"How hot is it out there right now?"

"Oh, a hundred three-four-five, something like that."

"And what is the body temperature of these men they bring up?"

"It varies too—around one hundred ten, I would say."

"I thought the long line slowed down, this being an election year—this heel tendon business and all."

"It probably has. But let us remember that these men are keyed up. No one tells them to slow down, so they aren't sure. Pressure on these men in the field is like pressure on an inner tube inside a casing. That pressure should never be released all at one time, but drained off gradually. You got to take account of the nervous system of a man."

"In other words, the pace of a man should not be changed too rapidly?"

"Right! Another example of this is the factory man who has worked forty-five years on one job. Suddenly he retires, and dies within six months."

"Do many of these heat exhaustion and fatigue cases live through it?"

"About half and half, under these conditions and circumstances. The pitiful thing with those who do pull through is that they're never the same."

"How's that?"

"Well, they're kind of like men off death row, men whose sentences have been commuted to life imprisonment. Those death row men are never the same. There's something indescribable that takes place inside of them that seems to make even the most intelligent ones sort of giddy and silly. With these men who have been overcome by heat exhaustion, it's almost the same—only, instead of being strong physically like the death row men usually are, these are weak in body and think a lot like little children. The heat does something within their brains."

"What's the news on the grapevine these days?"

"Well, Captain Burr was transferred to Camp One from Seven Camp. He and his wife and Pattycake moved into the big house by Captain Jones's."

"That should have made Screamin' John sad!"

"Screamin' John was killed. Some convict stabbed him to death one night in the mess hall."

"Seems like a lot of them bite the hardwood floor in that mess hall. Do you know Johnnie Lee?"

"Oh yes. He's out trusty again."

"Good! I put that crazy little devil to work at the mule barn when I was down there. I never would put him out trusty—I felt that he wasn't ready again to accept that kind of responsibility."

"Did you like your job at Seven Camp?"

"Not particularly, but I enjoyed trying to help some of those poor bastards. Anyhow, being a long line rider was better than pulling a cotton sack. Gads, that's been three years. I didn't know then what I know now!"

"What is that?"

I changed the subject. "What is the scuttlebutt from One Camp?"

"Oh, the Bull is still riding long line. I understand that he's having quite a time of it now. The riding is different this election year than what he is used to."

"Where did they put Captain Rumblefinger when Burr moved in?"

"Captain Rumblefinger transferred to Tucker to take

Colebiscuit's position as assistant superintendent."

"That's just what we need," I groaned, "an assistant superintendent who can't read or write!"

"As long as his orders are clearly defined, Rumblefinger can get by most anywhere."

"Do you by any chance know Ardmore or Thirty-One?"

"Oh yes. I know every convict on this farm. That is, I know *of* them." Jimmy coughed lightly behind his hand and excused himself. "What do you want to know about Ardmore or Thirty-One?"

"How they're getting along. What they're doing. That kind of wild scandal."

"Well, they're both in the garden squad at the One Camp vegetable shack."

I thought about that for a moment, then asked, "Did they get injured or something? Captain Jones doesn't usually put men in that squad unless there's something radically wrong with them."

"They just needed a rest, I assume." He started to say more, but changed his mind.

"That's where Caveman and I will likely be going. I'd better find out who's riding that squad!"

"A man they call Eagle Beak, I think. He's an Indian from Hot Springs."

"Do you think Judge Berry will win this election?"

He looked at me as though he was sorry I'd ask that question. "I don't know," he answered, and hurried away.

"Whata y'all wanta see 'em about?" I heard the convict medic ask someone beyond the front picket.

"What'n hell dif'rence it make? Cap'n Jones sent me down. Now open the gate!"

"Ah'll have no rough stuff in heah," the medic said firmly.

When the Bull came in he walked to my bed and stood for a moment. He rubbed a gloved finger alongside his nose and looked from me to Caveman, then back to me. "Cap'n Jones sent y'all a message. Part o' it's from him an' part o' it's from me. If any speck o' this heel ten'on bus'ness leaks out'n this prison, y'all two peckerwoods air dead mammy-jammers." He again looked from one of us to the other.

Vividly I recalled a scene in the cotton fields not long before, and what the Bull had told me then. "Wheah air y'all from?" I asked him, deliberately putting a nasal inflection upon each word.

The change in my voice startled him. "Wheah am ah from? Why ah'm from Marked Tree, wheah else?"

"Wail, thet's awright," I said. "They ain't nobody no god-damn good from Marked Tree noways."

The afternoon that Caveman's mother came down for a visit they moved his bed to the far side of the lockup away from mine. I saw her vaguely as she came onto the front picket and walked behind the two-by-four bars and around the guardwalk. The best I could tell, she was a slender woman with tin-rimmed glasses and swept-back hair. She seated herself upon an inverted bucket and reached between the wooden bars to smooth down a lock of her son's hair. *We all have mothers,* I thought. *Whether they are living or dead, we have them. And no matter what course our footsteps take in life, a mother can always see some reason or justification. Why can't society be more like a mother? It wouldn't have to justify our actions, but it could look deeper to find out why. With a better knowledge of the inner workings of a convicted felon, man could bring together more closely and fairly that which is just and that which is merely legal. But man is too busy with his own small world. The sheriff has to hurry to keep some other appointment. The prosecuting attorney must tone his arguments to match the pseudo-will of those in the courtroom at his back. And the judge must remember his pals at the country club. Those pals are the men who direct and shape the aspiring politician's career and future.* Disgustedly I turned my eyes away from the mother and her son at the far side of the lockup. But I heard the mother cry.

"Well, what did she say?" I asked Caveman the moment we were alone again.

"She said she don't know jus' who to see 'r what to do, but thet she'd try."

"God bless your mother," I said, and stared at the ceiling until my thoughts became mixed and tired and I went to sleep.

CHAPTER XXI

W HEN the big man walked through the front picket gate and into the lockup, I thought that he had the silverest hair I had ever seen. He came in slowly, in almost a lumbering fashion, stopped a few feet away from my bed and surveyed the barrack room scene. The man had blue eyes and a ruddy complexion, and I noticed that the coat of the light gray suit he was wearing was rumpled and torn at one elbow. I also noticed that the brown suede shoes he had on his feet were ill-shaped and crusted around the soles with Arkansas gumbo.

He reminds me of a huge bear, I thought—*a polar bear lumbering awkwardly across the ice on a downhill grade!*

"Look at this, Jonathan," another man said, and I glanced in that direction.

The man who had spoken was small—a man with a sharp nose, quick snappy eyes, and black hair. I saw that his hair was combed straight back and well oiled.

And he reminds me of a bantam rooster, I told myself, *a*

*fighting little rooster that's picking and pecking and turning
and letting his presence be known at all times.*

"I'm not interested in that ol' stove," the big man said.
"I know it's been there since 'twenty-six. I wanta talk to these
boys here." He held out a large stubby hand and said confidently, "I'm Judge Jonathan Berry. I'm goin' to be your next
governor."

"Look at this crap on these beds," the little man called.
"That must have also been here since 'twenty-six!"

"I don't care about that, Elmer. I wanta visit a while with
these fellows." Aside to Caveman and me the judge said,
"Don't min' Elmer. He's my campaign manager. He sees
ever'thang."

"How did you find us?" I asked.

"Ol' Jonathan Berry has ways of findin' people. Now don't
you bother about that." He seated his big frame on an empty
bed next to mine. "Are you boys gettin' enough to eat?"

"Right now we are," I told him, "but hell only knows what
will happen after you leave."

The campaign manager came to the foot of Caveman's
bed and sat on the metal stead. He let one foot dangle
loosely and nodded to us. "I'm going to put this big man here
in the governor's seat in Little Rock, and you boys had better
listen well to what he has to say."

"The way you talk, they'd think you were goin' to be
governor!" the judge said. Then to us, "Nothin' is goin' to
happen to either of you. Ol' Judge Berry will see to that.
Now I want you men to look after Ol' Judge Berry and help
him cinch this election."

"In what way?"

"Well, as you fellows may know, I'm usin' the talkathon
in my campaign. It is a method whereby I purchase radio

time and set up a battery of telephones. I answer questions any Arkansas citizen calls in and asks me. It's kind of an endurance procedure, and right now the people are mostly asking me what I will do about the Arkansas State Penitentiary when I become governor. This prison's the main plank in my platform, as you boys probably know. Anyhow, I want you both to put on tape all that you know and have seen happen here. I want the people of this Great State of Arkansas to see and to feel and to understand the strong motivation it takes for any man to reach down and mutilate a part of his body. I want 'em to hear that strap swish as it falls through the air onto a helpless man. I want 'em to hear it crack. With that tape I can go on the air and win this election hands down."

I looked at the judge's hands and saw that he had knotted them into huge fists. "But what will happen to us if you lose?" I asked.

"I won't lose, but say that I should; I want the people of Arkansas to know the horrible shape their politics are in. I was born in this dear state, and so was my father and my grandfather and my great-grandfather before him. My great-grandfather fought for the right of this land to become the twenty-fifth state in the Union. My grandfather fought with the Confederate armies from Shiloh to Appomattox. My father fought as a state representative to make Arkansas's informal legislature a little more formal. And I'll fight too! I want the people of this great state to taste every boll weevil in every pot of blackeyed peas that's ever been served in this prison. I want 'em to freeze down here in the wintertime, to burn down here in the summer. I want 'em to sleep on the wire springs of a cot with no mattress, to feel the boot of a brutal camp warden, to smell the stench of rottin' flesh out under a blazin' sun. In short, I want the people of this dear state to know what in hell's goin' on in the Arkansas State Penitentiary!"

I now saw that the judge's knuckles were white as he gripped his hands into tighter fists. "But what will happen to us if you lose?" I repeated.

The little campaign manager stood up and paced the floor. "Go on, Jonathan, tell them about that."

"I'm goin' to, Elmer." The big man cleared his throat. "If I should lose this election, I promise you this: In this great state I have a spotless reputation. No man, now that I know you are down here and in this condition, will ever dare lay a hand upon either of you. They'd better not! And furthermore, I promise you this: When I win this election and am sworn into office as governor, one of my very first acts will be to sign a pardon for each of you."

"Can we have protection here at this hospital, starting today?"

"I'll have two state troopers come down and sit by your beds in alternating shifts. I guarantee you both that no harm will ever come to either of you in any way."

I held out my hand to the silver-haired man. "Mr. Berry," I said, "you've got a deal."

"What about you?" he asked Caveman. "Will you back him up on this story?"

I glanced at Caveman and saw that same glassy stare I had noticed before. "Did yer mammy ever have a n'old red rooster?" he asked the judge.

"Why yes," the big man stammered, "as a matter of fact she did have."

"Then theah's yer answer," said Caveman, and held out an awkward hand to the startled judge.

The state trooper turned on Radio Free Arkansas and I heard my voice. "I have been here at Cummins for almost three years. During that time I have seen men kicked and stomped, maimed, mutilated and even killed. Right at this moment a number of men lie buried in unmarked graves, and I lie here, along with another convict, our heel tendons severed by our own hands, forced to do so or face certain death." On and on the tape ran. Over and over the judge and the little campaign manager played it. And the judge raged and preached and commented. He became angry and stormed. He appealed to the decency of mankind. He retold the history of the Great State of Arkansas, and made it sound good. He appealed to the sons and daughters and the fathers, and beseeched them in the names of the mothers. He yelled and he cried and he begged, and again played the tapes. He dared anyone to run a full and impartial and true investigation of the Arkansas State Penitentiary.

"Is it true thet the cap'ns at Cummins an' Tucker steal cotton?" people called in on the talkathon and asked.

"It's gone somewhere," Mr. Berry flatly stated. "I plan to ask for an audit of all books and look at the records and weigh sheets."

"How much cotton did them cap'ns get?" someone else wanted to know.

"Right at this point, it's difficult for me to tell. I have the disadvantage of being only a gubernatorial candidate right now. Perhaps you should ask Mr. McWhitney that question, or Captain Jones at the state prison."

"How will this 'fect our taxes, all this cotton an' money missin' at Cummins?"

"Well, in any state economy money is needed to operate a prison. Usually this money is provided by a general appro-

priation from the overall tax fund—or state treasury. We
have in this state the advantage of a prison that is designed
to be self-supporting. So instead of funds goin' from Little
Rock to Cummins, funds are expected to go from the prison
into the general treasury. This has not happened durin' the
McWhitney reign. Actually, money has been taken from
the state treasury to provide for the prison! And what this
means is that your tax dollar is travelin' from Little Rock to
Cummins, and this is a tragic mismanagement of public
institutions and funds."

"What'll y'all do 'bout the hide in the Arkansas State
Penitentiary?"

"When I'm elected governor, I'll have to keep the strap in
the prison. I'll have to keep it until solitary cells are con-
structed whereby we can handle these men. But this I promise you, Mr. Arkansas Citizen: No convict will ever be hit
more than ten licks at one time, and while a convict is bein'
punished a qualified doctor will be standin' by to stop the
whippin' at any time."

"How y'all gonna catch them criminals thet steal the
cotton an' peas at Cummins Farm?"

"I have found," Mr. Berry said confidently, "that if one
gives a thief enough rope the thief will catch himself. And
down at Cummins Prison Farm the wardens have certainly
been havin' enough rope. We don't know exactly yet which
ones they are, but they're all under close watch and are
practically caught already."

"What day did they take it?" a meek little voice piped.

"I don't know."

"Mr. Berry, ah been thankin' 'bout y'all gonna have them
books audited at the state prison. Now, thet's my line. Ah'm
a bookkeeper an' thet sorta thang. Have been since my wife
an' me got married in 1906. An' ah been thankin' thet maybe

they ain't got no records down theah—like weigh sheets, fer instant."

"You've made a good point, sir. However, we can determine the approximate amount of cotton taken from Cummins Prison Farm by estimatin' the overall gross poundage per acre. For instance, we know that a certain type of soil will produce an average amount of cotton in a given year. We can compare, say for last year, production at Cummins with a cross section of other acreages throughout that same area. The amount of cotton, of course, depends upon the type of cotton—whether long or short staple, the method of cultivation, and the annual rainfall. Then by knowin' the number of bales per acre that gumbo produced, we have only to count the acres under cultivation and multiply by the number of bales. Based on the price of cotton per pound in the year in question, we can come up with two money figures: The amount that should have stayed at Cummins for operatin' expenses, and the amount that should have gone into the state treasury."

"Can y'all do thet with peas, too?"

"We can come close."

"But what if it is awful close? It'd still be stealin'!"

"Detective Lint at Arkadelphia has already given me his complete confidence that he can solve even that."

"Thank y'all, Mr. Berry."

"You're a thousand times obliged."

"Mr. Berry, when me an' my husban' was fixin' a wagon wheel over on State Road 15 out'n Nanchez we saw a man with a load o' cotton haulin' it towards the gin at Sicily Island, an' ah jus' tol' my husban' thet somepin' didn't look right. Thet man jus' looked like he had somepin' up his sleeve."

"I can't say about that instance, ma'am, but this I promise

you, here on this talkathon for all the people of Arkansas to hear: When I'm elected governor, I will personally appear before the Arkansas legislature and fight for a bill that will make it legal for us to stop all wagons on any road in this dear state and investigate them. Cotton stealin' in Arkansas must stop!"

Another lady called in from a predestinarian Baptist Church. "Ah've jus' been thankin', an'—firs' let me ask y'all, Mr. Berry, is it true thet men are murdered an' buried in un-marked graves on Cummins Prison Farm?"

"I plan to look into that. When I become governor, I plan to run a full investigation on every phase of the information handed me concernin' Cummins Farm."

"Wail, as ah were sayin', what's gonna happen to the poor souls o' them men in unmarked graves? How will they be foun'?"

The big man cleared his throat, and I heard a telephone scrape on a table in the studio. "We have in our natures a re-markable capacity for bein' able, no mattter where we are, to bridge that gap between our mundane existence and the heavenly sublime. So I don't worry about the souls of those men, but I am concerned as to whether those bodies were legally buried where they are or not."

"Thank y'all, Mr. Berry. Ah jus' al'ays wondered 'bout thet."

"Not at all."

"Mr. Berry, y'all tol' someone on yer program thet y'all could tell cotton production by rainfall. Wail, ah work fer the weather bureau an' ah jus' thought ah'd call in an' let y'all know thet the rainfall in thet area over Cummins Farm is diff'rent from other parts o' Arkansas."

"Thank you, sir, for lettin' me know."

The judge and the little campaign manager again played the tape. "I have been here at Cummins for almost three years. During that time I have seen men kicked and stomped, maimed, mutilated and even killed. Right at this moment a number of men lie buried in unmarked graves, and I lie here, along with another convict, our heel tendons severed by our own hands, forced to do so or face certain death."

"Mr. Berry, ah'm Cherry Lynn an' ah'm in the second grade an' go to school at Texarkana Junior High an'—"

"You're in the second grade and you're in high school!"

"No—no, Mr. Berry. Ah jus' go to the high school 'cause the grade school burnt down when Gran'ma was goin' theah an' they ain't had time to fix it yet."

"Bless your heart, honey. When I'm elected governor I'll build you a new school. Now what is your question, Cherry Lynn?"

"Wail, ah jus' wonder couldn't they put someone out'n the fiel' to watch them mean ol' McWhitney men so they couldn't steal all our cotton?" She was crying.

"We'll work out something like that, Cherry Lynn. Now don't you worry your pretty little self one bit. Thank you for callin'."

"B-but, Mr. Berry, how do y'all know ah'm purty?"

"I can tell by the sound of your voice, sweetheart—good-bye."

"Judge Berry, I'm only an out-of-stater stranded here in Arkansas, but I've been here long enough to be a registered voter. I work for the National Foreign Aid Program for the Local Underprivileged and Mismanaged Statehoods, and I can't figure out why the majority of the people calling in on your talkathon is so worried about cotton thefts and embezzlements. We underwrite your cotton crops, even in those instances where cotton dominates politics as well as your economy. Now I'm amazed by this fact: I have noticed that here in Arkansas your criminals can kill your sons and rape your daughters, but woe be unto them if they tamper with your cotton production. They'd better not touch that man's wallet as he returns from the gin! . . ."

"Do y'all thank he's gonna be 'lected?" the state trooper sitting by my bed asked me.

"I do indeed," I answered, and I was right. The country people and those in the cities alike went into a rage about the missing cotton on Cummins Farm. They came from the northwest country, from the apple orchards and the poultry farms and the fertile lands. They came from the Ouachita Mountain region, men and women with quaint manners of speech and a love of legend and country music. From the valley of the Arkansas River they came, from the oil fields and the cattle ranches of the gulf plains. They swarmed from the river bottoms of the Mississippi, from the cotton and rice plantations and hog farms. There were old ones and young ones and little children. They rode down the hills and out of the bottoms in wagons and pushcarts, and one young fellow even came to the polls on a frail stick horse. They argued and they sang and they held stern faces. And out of the horde that flocked to the polls there was one common theme: "Nobody's gonna steal my cotton an' get by with it!"

"Y'all can't vote," a henchman said at the polls.

"Ah'm from Fort Smith an' ah've al'ays been from Fort Smith, an' my great-gran'pappy brought the firs' stern-wheeler up the Arkansas River in 1822, an' he fought ally-gaters an' san'bars an' snags an' had one helluva time, an' ah'n vote if ah want to!"

And the day after the election Radio Free Arkansas blared the news. "Berry wins—Berry wins—Berry wins!"

And the newspapers across the state went wild. In giant headlines they presented the news in no uncertain terms: JUDGE JONATHAN BERRY WINS BY NARROW

VICTORY, and the people paused, and then stopped and became thoughtful.

"The McWhitney machine is still strong in the State o' Arkansas."

"The fact thet Berry won won't brang back none o' thet cotton they took."

"Maybe we jus' won a fool's vict'ry an' shouldn't 'a voted atall."

And in the hospital barrack, I too paused for a moment of silent meditation. *Life,* I mused, *sometimes hangs on the very narrowest of circumstances.*

"Ah can have ya some braces fixed, Dardanelle," the medic told me. "Ah made 'em down in Mississippi when them ol' thangs couldn't hardly walk atall. Heah, see? Y'all jus' take Monel metal an' bend it aroun' this away an' it'll hol' yer heel up off'n the floor. A little later you'n toss 'em away, after yer ten'ons get loosened up some. You'n take these braces an' one crutch an' walk purty good."

A trusty called from somewhere beyond the front picket. "Dardanelle, looks like yer man won!"

"Wail, take it easy," the troopers said, and packed up their gear to return to Little Rock.

"Just a minute. I thought you fellows were going to stay down here until my pardon comes through."

"Ain't no need. Berry jus' tol' us to stay 'til he's 'lected. He said we'n come back after thet."

"Well, all right," I conceded. "Thank you for what you've done."

"Do y'all thank we're awright now?" Caveman asked me.

"If we use our heads, I do. Now, we are beginning to be able to walk fairly well, and they're going to be kicking us out of this hospital most any day. Our pardons cannot possibly come through before Berry is sworn into office, so we've got to stay one jump ahead of them. I want you to remain here and I'll go to Camp One and test the water. I'll have the medic call Captain Burr to come take me over there and, if everything is all right, I'll send a message saying 'The water is fine' and you come down. If everything isn't all right at One Camp, it's best that you stay here as long as they'll let you, and get any possible messages out. That's all we can do."

"Do y'all really thank thet's necessary? Why can't ah go with ya?"

"Maybe it isn't necessary, but it's an added precaution. Regardless whether it's necessary or not, it's a good show. It'll be noticed by Captain Jones, and will also help to keep us alert. In this state of excitement after the election we don't want to fall into the trap of forgetting ourselves."

"Wheah y'all goin' when y'all get yer par'on?"

"Hell, I don't know. Maybe to the Arbuckle Mountains of Oklahoma and start a pig farm."

"Can ah go with ya?"

I looked sharply at the black-haired man who had somehow touched on my life and, for a brief moment at least, become an essential part thereof. "Would you want to?" I asked, not knowing what else to say.

"Yeah."

"What about your mother and brothers in Waco? Wouldn't you want to go out there?"

"No. Thet's why ah went in them Ozark Mountains in the firs' place. Ah wanted to get away from 'em."

"Hog farming is rough these days, I understand." I was desperately trying, in this new turn of events, to find a way to handle the tricky situation.

"In them Arbuckle Mountains 'r whatever y'all call 'em we could get Polan' China sows, Chester White boars an' Duroc shoats. Ah could feed 'em, an' we could grow small patches o' corn an' give 'em good acorns to eat. We'd make lotsa money doin' thet."

"Let me think about it, Caveman. Let me think."

The mousy little convict eased up to me and smiled shyly. "Dardanelle, I just want to tell you that it's been a real pleasure having someone to talk to up here."

"I feel the same way, Jimmy."

"Well, I'm sorry we met under these circumstances, but I would rather that we did meet like this than not to have met at all."

"That's a fine compliment. It makes me feel good." I looked deeply into his eyes. "It really does, Jimmy. And I want to tell you this. If I'm ever up in Milwaukee I won't hesitate for a moment to look you up."

"Don't bother," he said, and he lowered his eyes and looked at the hardwood barrack floor.

"Why not?" I asked, surprised.

"I won't be there."

"But that's your home."

"I know it is, but I'm serving life and ninety-nine years here on Cummins Farm."

CHAPTER XXII

ACROSS Arkansas, in the shacks and the shanties and clapboard houses, small state officials tossed on their beds and slept fitfully. When morning came, they walked in their shorts to their oilcloth-covered tables and searched frantically through stacks of papers. They took the notes from one pile and placed them in another. They looked carefully about their rooms and saw their sleeping wives. They hurriedly bathed and put on their rumpled suits. Nervously they smoothed down their coat pockets with stiff sweaty palms and inspected themselves in cracked hand mirrors. Then they went to their doors and, smiling broadly, stepped awkwardly out into the chill autumn air of Arkansas politics.

Captain Jones on Cummins Prison Farm did none of these things. In the imposing residence below One Camp he lay still and slept soundly. When morning came, he walked in his bathrobe to his bedroom desk and absently signed a few papers. He took the papers and placed them in a portfolio.

He glanced across the room and half smiled at the young woman asleep in his bed. He bathed leisurely and put on a tailored suit. Casually he adjusted his tie and inspected himself in a full-length wall mirror. Then he went to his front door and, wiping any trace of the half smile from his features, he stepped calmly out into the chill autumn air of the Arkansas State Penitentiary.

It was late fall when Captain Burr came to the hospital for me. On the two braces the medic had fashioned, and the one crutch, I eased past the screen door and out onto the front porch. I stopped for a moment and looked at the new day. The sun was shining and tufts of white clouds lay high in the western sky, but the air was chill and over the fields was the first hint of oncoming winter. I shivered and pulled the blue jumper the little orderly had given me closer about my neck and shoulders. Then I worked my way down the hospital steps and out to the waiting jeep.

In the long years since Seven Camp days, Captain Burr had not changed. He was still the short stubby little man I remembered so well. On his face was the usual growth of heavy beard, and tobacco juice still ran down his chin and fell on his shirt front. For a while he drove and said nothing. But when we were halfway back to One Camp, he hunched his shoulders behind the wheel and spat out a side window. He hacked noisily and cleared his throat. "We gonna get along, ain't we, Dardanelle?"

"We always have, Captain Burr."

"Y'all ain't gonna say nothin' 'bout no cotton, air ya?"

"Why should I? It didn't belong to me."

"Cap'n Jones say y'all done too much talkin' up theah in thet hospital."

"So?"

He again hunched his shoulders and spat out the side window. "Oh, it's awright. Ah didn't mean nothin' 'bout thet. Ah jus' meant y'all ain't gonna say nothin' 'bout me, air ya?"

"Are you talking about when the trial begins in U.S. District Court?" I bluffed.

He glanced quickly at me. "Y'all mean they gonna try me?"

"If you don't be good to my buddy and me they might."

He looked straight ahead and said nothing more until we reached One Camp. "Cap'n Jones wants to talk to y'all 'fore ya go down to the veg'table shack."

"Dardanelle," the superintendent said, swiveling his chair from the window to face me, "how y'all been?"

"My health was discussed on Radio Free Arkansas, Captain Jones. Weren't you listening?"

"Oh, ah don't pay no 'tention to them thangs. Thet's politics. Ah gotta prison to run."

"How are you making out?"

"Wail, mos' o' the cotton's still in the fiel'," he said casually. "Thet don't mean much though—jus' thet we'll get it out in February 'stead o' December, an' the ditches won't get dug quite so deep in the sprang." He fiddled idly with an item of torture he picked up from his desk.

"What do you have on your mind, Captain Jones? You didn't call me up here to hash over old times."

He leaned back in his chair and looked directly into my eyes. "Ah still want y'all to ride this One Camp long line."

I couldn't believe what I was hearing. "Why?" I asked quietly.

He swiveled around to look out the window. "Wail, the Bull has reached the end o' his ridin' days an', frankly, ah ain't got nobody else out theah right now thet can do the job."

"Captain Jones, do you mean to tell me that after I've bucked you and your method and system with every ounce of my being—that you would still hand me a gun and the reins of a horse and put me in full charge of this prison camp!"

He continued to look out the window. "Ah thank it'd be awright if y'all tol' me it would. This ten'on bus'ness don't mean nothin'. Ah had other men tried to brang down heat on the joint before, but they didn't get nowheah. Ah also had men like Jonathan Berry, an' they didn't las' long. They jus' served their two-year terms an' disappeared. Thangs'll get back to normal in a few months. Right now ah need y'all to he'p me get this cotton crop out'n the fiel'."

"What about the maiming and stomping and killing?"

"Oh, them little wardens get pushed out'n shape sometimes. Ah'll have to jack 'em up an' they'll be awright."

"How will you get the men to pick cotton when you can't use the strap?"

"Ah'n use the strap," he said, and swung back to face me. He looked at his desk. "Ah jus' gotta be careful right now to on'y hit ten licks, but nobody tol' me ah can't hit thet ten licks forty times a day."

"And what is the food like now? Is it still the weevils and peas?"

"Ever'thang's jus' like it was. The on'y dif'rence is thet we gotta go easy on thet strap."

"My answer is *no*, Captain Jones. I will not ride your long line."

"Why?"

"Do you want me to really tell you why?"

"Go on, Dardanelle."

"Well, to begin with, I think you are making a big mistake here on Cummins Farm. I don't approve of a prison system of this type, but since this is what you have it can be a better thing. These men will work with a minimum of punishment if you will decently feed them and give them some incentive. On this type of prison farm you can raise all the food that twenty times this population can eat, and you can give the men reductions in sentences for any cotton they pick above and beyond their regular tasks. You can give each man a clean suit of clothing to wear twice a week, and you can wash their dirty ones. You could give your trusties added merits for sanely guarding these men, and you could operate this prison without fear—no matter who the governor happened to be."

"But the people want these men punished at hard labor!"

"Poppycock! The people of this state couldn't care less. Besides, there's nothing easy about picking cotton, no matter how one does it. Just staying here is punishment. Give these men a decent prison and you can ride on that achievement to the governor's office in Little Rock."

"Thet's somepin' ah never wanted to do is to be guv'ner. 'Sides, we wouldn't make no money down heah operatin' like thet."

"The hell you wouldn't. You'd make more than you're making now. Look at the time you lose mollycoddling this prison through election years. Fire those stupid wardens you've got and get some men with sense and reason. Pay them more and you'll make more. This farm, as much as I disapprove of it, can actually be in this day and age an exemplary prison within these United States. And you're a shrewd enough man to do it, Captain Jones."

The superintendent looked at me and I saw that his gray eyes were no longer mysterious. They were kind eyes, and a little sad, and I saw that somewhere down deep in them there was a hint of fear. "Ah'm too tard anymore, Dardanelle." He stood up and leaned heavily on his desk. "Ah gotta bad heart. Y'all shoulda come down this away back in the thirties. Y'all stay heah at One Camp with me, Dardanelle, an' we'n fin' someone else to go ride thet long line."

"I'll stay here at the camp, Captain Jones, but not with you. And neither will I help you get anyone else to ride that long line. You are the superintendent on Cummins Farm, not I."

He again sat down and composed himself. He looked sharply at me and I saw that his gray eyes had changed. Now they were cold and hard and mysterious eyes and the kindness was gone. "Awright, Dardanelle, heah's what ah decided fer y'all. 'Slong as y'all stay inside this guardline heah on the campgroun' nobody's gonna touch ya 'r say nothin' to ya. You'n stay 'round the veg'table shack in the daytime an' sleep in the barrack at night. You'n thresh a few peas if ya want to, but y'all don't even hafta do thet if va don't want. Y'all jus' stay out'n my bus'ness an' ah'll stay out'n yourn."

"What about Caveman, Captain?"

"What 'bout Caveman?" he asked irritably.

"Will you put him on this camp yard and leave him alone also?"

"If thet's what y'all want, Dardanelle."

"Will you send a little warden to get him—right now, this moment?"

"Yes—yes," he half yelled and waved his hand at the door. "Now y'all get out'n heah an' leave me alone. Y'all take up nine tenths o' my time an' ah'm tard o' fartin' with ya!"

CHAPTER XXIII

LOCATED on the back side of the camp yard, the vegetable shack was a small simple building with two rooms and a dirt floor. In one of the rooms was an old firebox cookstove, and in the other a deep sink for washing turnips and peas brought in from the fields. The vegetable shack squad, or garden squad, consisted of some twelve to fifteen men—the lame and the old and the whimpering. In the lax days of election years, the man in the long line who whined the loudest went to the vegetable shack. "The wheel thet squeaks the noisiest gets the mos' grease," the other men sighed, and continued to pick the cotton in the icy cold.

"All they got in thet squad anyways is a bunch o' finks," someone said.

"They got Dardanelle an' Caveman in thet squad. Y'all better watch what yer sayin'. They ain't no snitches 'r finks."

"Yeah, ah know, but thet's dif'rent. They gotta reason to be theah."

"Did y'all see thet crazy Caveman? He's gone an' made

'em a cave under the woodpile. He jus' took some chunks an' dug down deep an' set 'em up edgewise an' made 'em a cave. Stays in it all o' the time while he ain't in the barrack. Chris', is he ever weird!"

"Ol' Dardanelle ain't no slouch hisself. Since he quit shavin' he looks like Long John Silver 'r somepin'."

" 'Specially on thet one crutch an' them braces."

"Did y'all see thet crazy bastard come through the mess hall the other day? The way them Monel braces was poundin' the floor he sounded like a herd o' elephants. Damn, he looks tall on them braces!"

"Them guys air both nuts."

"They might be nuts but they ain't out heah in this ice an' snow pickin' cotton!"

"No, ah'll give 'em credit fer thet. An' Burr an' Jones shore don't bother 'em neither."

"Hell, they afraid to! Even crazy, Ol' Dardanelle can thank circles 'round any warden on Cummins Farm."

"Shore takes guts to do what they done."

"It don't take no guts. Ya jus' gotta be crazy."

"Well, whatever it is ah shore wisht ah was a little bit like thet. My hands air gonna get frostbite an' come off out heah."

A huge woodpile, comprised of some one hundred and fifty cords of split oak, was situated halfway between the vegetable shack and mess hall. The bright new wood was piled high in pell-mell fashion, and it was directly to this part of the camp yard that Caveman headed when he came down from the hospital barrack. Expertly he dug into the huge pile. He threw pieces of oak right and left. For a week he worked, hour after hour, from morning to night. He calculated the area needed, and he measured it off with outstretched hands. He stepped to the right, and he stepped to the left, and when he had finished the result of his labor was a walk-under cave, or dugout. It was in this small enclosure that Caveman spent most of his time, while I spent mine sitting on top of the great mound.

"Ah'm Eagle Beak. Ah'm from Hot Springs. Why don't y'all men c'mon in the veg'table shack wheah it's warm?"

I looked at the man who had spoken and saw that he was a big Indian. His hair and eyes were jet black, his complexion dark brown, his waistline full and large and extended out and over a cracked leather belt with a loose end. I looked again at the man's face and saw why they called him Eagle Beak. His nose was large and curved like that of an eagle— out and abruptly downward, over a very small mouth.

"You're the garden squad rider, aren't you?"

"Thet's right. Whyn't y'all men c'mon in an' 'joy the fire? We gotta good one goin' in thet cookstove."

"If it gets too cold for us out here, I'll set the goddamn woodpile on fire," I told him.

The big Indian fidgeted and rubbed the long hair on the back of his neck. "Cap'n Jones tol' me to he'p make y'all men comfor'ble out heah. Now we ain't doin' no work much 'round the shack. The veg'tables air out'n the fiel' an' they's jus' a few peas to wash an' some turnips to trim."

"Did Captain Jones also tell you that Caveman and I aren't doing any more work as long as we're on Cummins Farm?"

"No—no, ah didn't mean thet! They ain't much 'round the shack to do noways. Ah jus' thought thet if y'all wanta come in ah'd go down 'long them creek banks an' set out some traps fer rabbits. We'n all have plenty o' rabbits to eat this winter."

Caveman immediately came from under the woodpile.

"Can ah clean 'em?" he asked, and I noticed that glassy stare in his ₙyes.

The Indian shrugged. "Ah don't care if ya clean 'em. Save me o' havin' to get my hands in the bloody mess."

And so, all that winter Eagle Beak ran his traplines and Caveman skinned out the catch. On the old stove in the vegetable shack, Ardmore and I did the cooking. Thirty-One stoked up the fires, and during that winter we had jack rabbit, swamp rabbit, and cottontail rabbit. We ate rabbits with ears one third their body length, Arctic rabbits of the snowshoe variety, European rabbits who were just passing through, and one scroungy little bunny who drifted in with the snows from Oklahoma, and Hoover days. Then they were gone.

"What'll we do?" a lanky man asked.

"Hell, I don't know. I was beginning to get filled up on rabbits anyhow."

"Ah feel guilty," someone said. "Thet one rabbit ah ate looked like Bugs Bunny!"

Everyone laughed.

"No wonder these turnips air so pithy."

"Why's thet?"

"Them rabbits pithed on 'em."

"Thet's a good one," the lanky man said, and slapped his leg. "Do any o' y'all know what the little cottontail rabbit were doin' in the Westin'house 'frigerater?"

"No, what?"

"He were westin'."

"Wail, it's gettin' on towards sprang an' we gotta go to work," said Eagle Beak. "We gotta clean off some groun' an' get some kinda garden planted."

Ardmore jumped up. "Now jus' a cotton-pickin' minute, Ol' Eagle Beak Rider. Don't you realize thet these men air crazier'n hell 'bout y'all?"

"How's thet?" the rider asked.

"Wail, they come to 'pend on you fer their vittles."

The Indian glanced suspiciously at Ardmore. "What y'all gettin' at?"

"He's gettin' hungry ag'in," the lanky man said.

"Yeah, he's gettin' hungry," agreed Thirty-One.

The Indian tightened his belt. "Ah can't get y'all nothin' to eat. They ain't no more rabbits to catch!"

I looked at Ardmore and Thirty-One. "Come to think about it," I said, "what in hell are you two birds doing out here in this vegetable shack squad anyhow?"

"Y'all mean ya don't like us out heah?" asked Ardmore.

"No—no, it isn't that. I couldn't care less whether you're out here or somewhere else. I just happened to remember that the hospital orderly told me you were in this squad, and I wonder why."

"Wail," said Ardmore, "ah thank Cap'n Jones thought maybe we'd do somepin' like y'all done, cut our ten'ons 'r somepin'."

"So you and this runty sidekick of yours have ridden out here through the blood of Caveman and me! You two didn't have guts or imagination enough to make it out here on your own accord!"

"Y'all want us to go back to the long line, Dardanelle?"

"Oh no, not now. You're part of Captain Jones's business, so I won't bother you. I want you to know, however, that I think you're both two gutless sonofabitches, and that I don't like your class of people."

Caveman picked up a turnip knife. "Do y'all want me to kill 'em, Dardanelle?"

"Y'all men air mad," Eagle Beak said. "All them rabbits have jumped aroun' in ya an' now yer hungry ag'in an' wanta fight. Gi' me thet knife, Caveman." The rider moved forward.

The glassy stare came into Caveman's eyes and he backed away to a corner. He said nothing, but continued to hold the knife with the point out, and to look at the Hot Springs Indian.

I edged between the two men and spoke quietly to Eagle Beak: "I wouldn't go any closer if I were you," and the rider stopped. His face paled and he seemed to realize that death was not far away.

I turned to Caveman. "If you kill him you can't go with me to those Arbuckle Mountains."

Expertly Caveman flipped the knife into a post a few inches away from Eagle Beak's head. The steel blade tore into the oak wood and the handle vibrated.

"Tell us a story," I said to Ardmore. "We've got more tension in this vegetable shack than we have smoke from that old cookstove!"

"Wail, it were down to Seven Camp a few years back, an' the science blood people use to come an' take blood. They'd pay us convicts fi' bucks fer ever' pint thet we'd let 'em siphon off, an' they didn't care how many. Wail, ever'one down theah used to gamble, an' the moneymen in the barrack would loan cash to anybody fer two bits back on a dollar. An' ever'one was in debt to the moneymen. Wail, this one ol' thang called Strangbean, he shore liked to gamble, an' he was in debt up to his rumpus, but he al'ays managed to pay back ever'thang he had owin'. So the moneymen tol' 'em, 'Strangbean, we know yer awful good fer yer pay, an' thet's why we like ya. Therefore, when them science blood people come down, y'all better get out theah an' sell a lotta blood 'r we gonna fix ya.'"

"If they liked 'em so much, what was they gonna fix 'em fer?" the lanky man asked.

"Oh, ah don't know," said Ardmore, "thet's jus' part o' the story. Anyways, thet's what Ol' Strangbean done. When thet bloodwagon got parked on the Seven Camp yard, the firs' man up theah was thet ol' skinny Strangbean. 'What's yer type?' the science blood people asked, an' Strangbean said, 'Ah don't know. Ah al'ays tried to be a purty good feller.' Wail, the science blood people decided the on'iest thang to do were to test Ol' Strangbean an' fin' out what weight his blood were. 'Ah thank it's twenty weight,' one o' 'em said, but after a while they come to the conclusion thet Strangbean had the rarest blood they ever saw. It was triple-aught-pea-soup 'r somepin' like thet. Anyways, one o' them science blood people foun' some boll weevils in Strangbean's blood an' wasn't gonna take it. 'Ah jus' gotta sell some,' Ol' Strangbean pleaded. 'Ah al'ays pay my debts, an' them moneymen air gonna kill me if ah don't.' The science blood people looked at him. 'We'n give ya four bucks a pint,' they said, 'but thet's all we'n go. Too many weevils an' not 'nough weight. We'll take all ya wanta sell fer thet price, though.' Wail, Ol' Strangbean done some quick figurin' fingerwise an' tol' 'em they could start out by takin' three pints. An' thet's what they done. They took three pints."

"They shore did," said Thirty-One. "Ah remember it jus' like it were yesterday. Ah sol' two pints thet day myself."

"Wail, anyways, them science blood people siphoned three pints out'n Ol' Strangbean an' he got up an' kinda shook hisself an' decided he still felt purty good. 'Ah believe ah'n go another'n 'r two,' he tol' the science blood people. 'Heah, take it out'n this arm this time.' So they siphoned off two more pints, an' Ol' Strangbean got up an' kinda staggered toward the mess hall, but the moneymen got 'em. 'Hell, y'all can't pay us all ya owe with jus' twenty dollars. You still owe us six.' So Strangbean stumbled aroun' in a circle an' headed back up wheah the science blood people was. 'Heah come thet triple-aught-pea-soup man ag'in,' someone said. 'Thet stuff he's got is awful weevilly an' we're scrapin' the bottom o' the barrel. We better jus' give 'em three bucks a pint from now on.' So Ol' Strangbean sol' two more pints an' thet made seven, but he paid back ever'thang he had owin'. Thet's why them moneymen liked 'em so well. He al'ays give 'em back ever'thang they had comin'."

"He shore did," said Thirty-One.

The lanky man shook his head. "How could he sol' seven pints? Thet's 'bout all a human bein' got in 'em."

"Don't ferget," said Ol' Ardmore, "we had weevils an' peas fer supper thet night. Ol' Strangbean built it all back awright."

I looked at Caveman, then at Eagle Beak. "The tension's still strong in here. Tell us another one, Ardmore."

"Hell, ah can't thank o' no more right now, Dardanelle. Ah'm tard."

"Well, you'd better do something."

"Ah'n sang 'em a boll weevil song ah made up, if that'll he'p."

"Ah don't wanta heah no boll weevil song," said Eagle Beak.

Ardmore looked at me and shrugged. "Then they'll jus' hafta kill each other, ah guess. . . ."

"We've got to think of some way to get food," I told Eagle Beak a few days later. "Caveman's getting awfully hungry."

"Ah'n get a fat hog over to Cap'n Jones' pen," the rider suggested. "Ah'n hook a mule to the veg'table squad wagon an' brang it in."

"Ah'n go he'p 'em," the lanky man said.

"Can ah clean it?" asked Caveman.

Eagle Beak shrugged his shoulders. "Ah don't give a damn if y'all clean it. The on'y thang is, we gotta run mos' o' the meat up to the mess hall to keep the yardman quiet. But ah'n al'ays get more when we need 'em."

And so, all that early spring Eagle Beak brought in the Hampshires and Caveman butchered them out. With the turnip knife the mountain man stabbed deeply into the steaming innards of the smelly creatures. Across the vegetable shack floor ran blood from the deep hog caverns, and that blood mixed with the loose dirt and became mud. Caveman seemed to delight in the gory mess of his job, and Ardmore and I delighted in cooking any pork cut for any man, no matter the size or shape.

"Get this fire stoked up," I told Thirty-One. "This is good pork liver and I am going to roast it."

"Ah like the kidneys," the lanky man said. "They remin' me o' when ah was back in the Ouachita Mountains at Pencil Bluff. Mamma an' Daddy used to kill hogs an' ah jus' loved to cook the kidneys in the hot ashes."

"Here," I said, and threw him a couple of large ones from a giant boar.

The yardman came to the vegetable shack and snooped around like a whipped dog. "How much meat can ah get fer the long line today?"

"Whatever you'n fin' thet we ain't eatin'," Eagle Beak said. He pulled an entrail from a steaming pile and stripped it between thumb and forefinger. He then tilted his head to one side and fed the slimy mess into his mouth.

The yardman looked at the rider and wrinkled his nose. "How do y'all eat them thangs?"

The rider shrugged.

"Ah'n cook 'em, Eagle, if y'all want me to."

"Not fer me, Ardmore. Ah like 'em raw, right out'n the belly."

"When air the par'ons comin' through?" Caveman asked me one day. "Thet guy Berry were sworn in las' January an' heah it is March."

"Beats me," I said, "but I think they will. It just takes a little time for the red tape to get cleared away and the papers to come through. Now, the thing for us to do is to get that gut-eater out to the pigpen again for another good Hampshire shoat."

"Do ah get to keep cleanin' 'em?"

"You most certainly do. Why do you like that job so well?"

"Ah don't know, but ah could butcher our hogs when we get up to them Arbuckle Mountains."

"Caveman," I asked, "what do you remember most about your early childhood?"

"What y'all askin' me thet fer?"

"Oh, I don't know. I guess I just wondered."

"Wail, ah remember one time ah was out'n the yard. Ah was 'bout six years ol' an' they was a lot o' girls out theah playin'. They wouldn't play with me though, so ah jus' thought ah'd show 'em how important ah were an' ever'-thang. So ah caught one o' Mamma's ol' red roosters an' cut off a wing. Lord, thet thang bled."

"Did it impress the girls?"

"Naw. After ah done thet they wouldn't even come close to me atall."

"What did you do about thet?"

"Nothin' much. Ah jus' caught the ol' rooster ag'in an' cut it all up in little pieces an' throwed it down in a ditch. Ah remember thet ah hated them girls fer not noticin' more."

I changed the subject. "Ol' Eagle Beak is getting nervous about this hog stealing business. I think he is ready to call it quits."

Caveman looked at me. "Le's kill thet sonofabitch an' put 'em in one o' them pickle barrels."

I glanced at a number of barrels half filled with salt water sitting in one corner of the vegetable shack. "We don't want to do that, Caveman. We'd never get out of this stinking rathole if we pulled some boo-boo of that kind. Besides, Eagle has been good to us. He caught rabbits last winter and he's stolen every hog on this farm. Let's leave him alone."

"Ah don't like 'em, an' even if y'all don't want to he'p me ah'm still gonna kill 'em."

"If you do, it's like I told you before. I won't let you go with me to those Arbuckle Mountains."

Caveman turned his head quickly and looked away. "Wail, even if ah don't kill 'em ah still don't like the loudmouthed bastard."

"Y'all rams c'mon out heah," five captains called one morning from the front picket. They called every man in the vegetable shack except Caveman and me. "Y'all mammy-jammers done stole ever' hog Cap'n Jones got. Get down theah."

The big strap rose and fell, and the eerie screams filled the concrete building. When they came to Eagle Beak, they hit him the hardest. "Oooooh, Cap'n!" he yelled. "Y'all tol' me to make Dardanelle an' Caveman comfor'ble!"

"Ah didn't tell ya to not plant a garden an' to steal Cap'n Jones' hogs!"

"Oooooh, Cap'n, ah won't steal no more hogs eeeever!"

"Ah know ya won't. They ain't no more goddamn hogs on this pea farm fer y'all to steal."

"Why air ya jus' whuppin' us an' not Ol' Dardanelle an' Caveman?"

"Hell, they ain't stole no hogs. They can't even get off'n the yard to go get any!"

CHAPTER XXIV

STATE OF ARKANSAS
Executive Department
PROCLAMATION

To all to whom these presents shall come, greetings:

Whereas, Ol' Dardanelle, white male, was convicted in Yell County of the crime of Forgery and Uttering and sentenced to a term of five years in the Penitentiary; and

Whereas, said Dardanelle should be released from the Penitentiary before the expiration of his maximum sentence; and

Whereas, the Board of Pardons, Paroles and Probation has recommended that subject's citizenship be restored;

Now, therefore, I, Jonathan Berry, by virtue of the power and authority vested in me as Governor of the State of Arkansas do hereby pardon Ol' Dardanelle of the above crime and restore to him all rights, privileges and immunities as enjoyed before passage of the above sentence.

This Proclamation is being granted without application being made to me by an attorney or paid representative of Dardanelle.

In testimony whereof, I have hereunto set my hand and caused to be affixed hereto the Great Seal of State in the Governor's Office, Little Rock, Arkansas.

Signed: Elmer Udial   Signed: Jonathan Berry
        Secretary of State   Governor

"Ah wanta go too!—Oh Gawd, ah wanta go too! Ah wanta go with Dardanelle!"

"The guv'ner on'y par'oned ya on killin' the ol' man. Y'all still got the state trooper sentence. Now you jus' get back under thet woodpile an' whimper. You'll be awright after a while."

I took off my braces and threw down my crutch. I limped quite badly and sometimes, uncontrollably, my feet pattered like those of a duck.

"You'n get a n'operation," someone said. "A special doctor can fix them feet up good as new."

"Maybe I'll go to San Francisco for that," I answered, and limped out of the prison and onto paved road 65 to Pine Bluff.

ABOUT THE AUTHOR

"I was born in Okmulgee County, Oklahoma, the fourth of seven children (five of them girls). My father was a Cherokee sandhill sharecropper, my mother an Irish brush-arbor churchgoer. During the Second World War I served in the Army Parachute Infantry. After my discharge I became a highway patrolman. Since then I've been, among other things, a grocery store manager, a construction superintendent, a laboratory technician, a peach thinner, a hitchhiker, a hobo, and a convicted hot check artist. Several years ago I gave up the call of the open road, married and settled in Rockford, Illinois. Today I consider myself an honest man in that I have a number of legitimate check-cashing cards which are honored in all Rockford stores."

K Wymand Keith served four years of a five-year sentence for forgery and uttering at Cummins Prison Farm. *Long Line Rider*, his first book, is based on what he saw and experienced there. He plans to continue writing and is well along with his second book.